Growing Up
in
God's Country

A Memoir

El McMeen

BookLocker

Table of Contents

Foreword

My friend Steve Baughman asked me once whether I ever thought of writing my memoirs. Steve was my sometime co-author[1], and a darned good guitarist and lawyer. I said I hadn't.

Later on, I thought about it. I've gone from the "God's Country" of rural Pennsylvania -- Lewistown and Huntingdon -- to Cambridge, Massachusetts, Philadelphia, PA, New York City, Mountain Lakes and Sparta, NJ, back to Huntingdon, and then back to Sparta. All of it is God's country, to be sure, with the devil and his minions lurking and working. If you don't believe in the devil, think again. And watch your back.

My journey hasn't involved many fancy, exotic places. I've never been to Monaco, Belize, Beijing, Tokyo, or even the Burning Man festival in the Nevada desert. (As to the latter, my dear friend and guitarist Larry Pattis wrote a great tune called "Burning Man;" maybe that counts.) Nevertheless, I've been blessed. God's hand has been all over the journey. Most of the time I was clueless. Then I started to get it.

---

[1] Objection! Overruled! (Or, Two Lawyers Have a Little "Chat" About God and Hell) ©Steve Baughman and E. Ellsworth McMeen, III (Booklocker.com, Inc. 2013)

Jesus said, as recorded in John 10:10:

"The thief [that is, the devil] does not come except to steal, and to kill, and to destroy. I have come that [you] may have life, and ... have *it* more abundantly." [Emphasis El's]

I continue to be amazed and grateful for the abundant life the Lord has given me, in family, law, music, ministry, and writing. I've had my share of the devil. He's part of the story, especially in my early years. Boys and girls, the fact that I've done stupid things doesn't mean I recommend them. ("Don't try this at home!") Nor does it mean that if you do them, you'll get a pass. Don't smoke; avoid destructive behavior; be kind.

Romans 8:28 says that not everything in life is good; not everything in life is God [or, at least, God's best]; but God causes all things to work together for good for those who love Him and are called according to His purpose [namely, to be like Jesus]. I thank Pastor Duane Sheriff of Victory Life Church in Durant, Oklahoma for that paraphrase. I add only that the Lord clearly protected me before I knew Him. Call it "common grace," call it whatever. That protection is a large part of my story.

Challenges for me started from Day 1 -- actually before Day 1 -- in June 1947. The Lord has gotten me through those challenges in ways that only an amazing Father could. The Lord has a great sense of humor, too. If you can't process that, consider the penguin, the lightning bug, and the frog.

I've not arrived, nor am I special. I'm definitely not grown up. That's why the title of this book is "growing up." (Even that may be inaccurate; my sense of humor may actually be regressing.) I do believe, however, that I am amazingly blessed of the Lord. You are or can be, too. I hope this book will lead you to consider your own life, and how the Lord has intervened, whether with thunder, with a still, small voice, or with some other crazy, wonderful "stuff."

El McMeen
Late 2018
Sparta, NJ

Franny and Sandy McMeen,
Atlantic City, NJ

1

Lewistown, PA

In 2006 I called my mother. She was 92 and bedridden, but still sharp. "Guess where I am," I bellowed into the cellphone. "I don't know, Sandy. I'll bite!" I continued yelling. "I'm at the Lewistown Hospital, looking at the room where you gave birth to me on June 3, 1947!"

I lied. I didn't really know where the delivery room was. I <u>was</u>, however, in the <u>parking lot</u> looking at that medical monolith on Electric Avenue, Lewistown, central PA, USA, Planet Earth.

We had a laugh over this, and went on to have a good visit at her home in Huntingdon, PA. It was to be our next-to-last time together. In 2007 she died. (Parenthetically, she hated the term "passed away." "Just say 'died,'" she would command.)

My nickname was Sandy. Anyone who knew me before age 16 calls me Sandy. It's only with an effort that they can say "El." I'll always be Sandy to them. The name apparently related to my blond hair. In later life my mother confessed the real reason: I had been conceived at the seashore. I can't verify that claim from date books, but must admit that my parents <u>did</u> visit Atlantic City in the relevant period. I guess they didn't spend all their time on the beach or at Steel Pier. My mother also asserted categorically that my sister had been ten months in utero, darkly implying that

1

Franny was somehow complicit in her delayed birth. Mother's friends pooh-poohed that, but Mother was a smart Cornell grad, and after all, it <u>was</u> her uterus.

We from Lewistown are the few, the proud, and in certain cases (although not mine) <u>actually</u> Marines. The population in Lewistown when I was born was 13,000, give or take. It was and is the County Seat of Mifflin County. As a result perhaps of declining industry, the population now consists of 8,000 or so stalwarts.

We natives of Lewistown are diverse but have two common battles. One is to convince people that the town is actually Lewis<u>town</u>, and not Lewis<u>burg</u>, where Bucknell University is located. "Oh, yes, Lewistown; I have a friend who goes to Bucknell!" One feels like a soul-crusher to have to correct such an enthusiast.

The other challenge -- all right, these are not "challenges" like Iwo Jima or world peace. The other <u>issue</u> is to indicate that it's not Lewis<u>ton,</u> as in Maine. It's "Lewis<u>town</u>," with a "w." Of course, by now, people have lost interest and are checking for text messages on their smartphones.

We from central PA tend to have some speech eccentricities. We may say "ontil" for "until," or "gawn" for "going." We may refer to you and your ilk as "youns," pronounced "yunz," with one syllable. We may say "the car needs fixed" instead of "the car needs <u>to be</u> fixed." (My wife Sheila likes to pounce on that one. I have tried to defend it, unsuccessfully.)

There are sometimes peculiar, local meanings to otherwise innocent words. If a fellow student in elementary school calls you "ignorant" (pronounced "ignernt"), that doesn't mean you are lacking knowledge but that you have a "dirty mind."

My mother had to admonish me regularly about "dropping my g's" when I would say "dew-un" rather than "do-ing." She was heard to say "iggle" for "eagle" more than once, so she wasn't clear of the local influence. In fact, she was nailed at Cornell for being from central Pennsylvania. One of her English professors was William Strunk, Jr., the original author of the iconic grammar book The Elements of Style. E.B. White would later expand the book greatly and add his imprimatur to it.

Strunk had the skill and reputation of being able to tell students where they were from after listening to them talk. Mother was up, and after she uttered a few words, Strunk pronounced that she lived within 35 miles of State College, PA! He was right, of course, almost to the mile. If we central PA types think that other people talk funny, well, we need to remember Strunk and Biddle (my mother's maiden name).

Back to the hospital. In later years I visited the hospital to distribute some of my Christian tracts in waiting rooms. I noticed a plaque with the names of the Presidents of the Hospital Auxiliary over the years. My mother Josephine served from 1950-52. She was listed as "Mrs. Elmer E. McMeen." I was going to engage in some grandiose societal analysis regarding men, women, and names back then, but quickly noticed that other women used their first names rather than their husbands' names, so whatever theory I might have had was wrecked.

Moving on. Lewistown was a great town in which to be a kid. It was, to be sure, cold in the winter, hot and humid in the summer, and oddly lacking in trees in various parts of downtown, giving those areas somewhat of a bleached look in the summer heat. A central square and monument graced the town. There were lots of theaters, cozy restaurants, great bike-riding places, teaberry ice cream, the river, and the Panthers as the high school football team (now the Mifflin County Huskies).

Most importantly, perhaps, for us 11-year-olds back then, there were various surreptitious places to smoke cigarettes pilfered from one's parents. If you wanted to be brazen and smoke out in the open, the graveyard by the high school was perfect. It was kind of spooky, and, of course, the residents didn't mind.

But I get ahead of myself. We need to return to the hospital. On June 3, 1947, there was a problem. I was born, to be sure, but when I emerged, the umbilical cord was wrapped around my neck four times, tightly. If I had not been born breech, I simply would not have survived. How do I know? The doctors said so.

Years later, as I would try to visualize that whole scene, I felt the Lord showing me, graphically, His hand in my mother's womb, gently turning me around 180 degrees so that I would exit rear-end first. You may say I have a vivid imagination, but I've had that vision several times. You may say I give undue credit to the Lord. I say, better that than the converse.

I was alive, but all was not well. I weighed in at 5 pounds, 3 ounces. My mother liked to tell people that I looked like a "picked chicken" and that it took many months for me to become "presentable."

But puniness was not the major problem. The cord had cut off oxygen to parts of my brain that control motor functions. The result was cerebral palsy. It was considered a "mild case," but it left me with coordination and stamina problems and, as I was to find out decades later, weakness on my left side, from the eye all the way down to the leg.

In 1953 our family doctor, Dr. John Hunter, consulted a Philadelphia physician, Dr. Frederic Leavitt, about me. (Dr. Leavitt's office on Pine Street in Philly was only a few blocks from the place where I was to live during my first term at Penn Law School 16 years later.)

Dr. Leavitt's letter states in part as follows:

"Mrs. McMeen brought Ellsworth to my office June 30, 1953. This little fellow is a case of 'cerebral palsy' - so called. He is really a case of retardation of cerebral brain stem and cerebellar development as a result of severe and constant anoxia due to interference with the blood supply of the brain prior to birth - due to the fact that the umbilical cord was apparently tightly constricting the neck for some time prior to his birth. [*Note from El: I guess lawyers aren't the only ones guilty of long sentences and big words.*] It was fortunate that he was delivered by breech instead of head presentation, because had it been the usual procedure he undoubtedly would have died at birth. Also, fortunately, the boy is not epileptic as many of these children tend to be nor is he particularly intellectually retarded."

5

My children and I have mused together about the significance of the word "particularly" in the last sentence of the quote. "Dad, does that mean you are 'generally' retarded?" Of course, the term "retarded" has gone out of fashion, but the joke was still good.

In the 1980's my mother sent me an article from the New York Times magazine that addressed the matter of so-called "mild" cases of cerebral palsy. The article concluded that there was no such thing. CP is CP. My mother agreed, and wrote the author of that article confirming his conclusions.

As mentioned, my nickname growing up was "Sandy." When I hit age 16, my mother suggested that "Sandy" was for kids, and "El" might be a better name. Maybe she was right, but I do have friends and contemporaries, like guitarist and educator Alexander ("Sandy") Shalk, who at least seem to be adults. That having been said, let's take a pause from names-and-games in Lewistown to look further at Sandy's "problem."

2

Irish Jigs in Central PA

As I now, in my early dotage, reflect on the physical problems of my youth, I praise the Lord that smartphones didn't exist back then. It might well have crushed my spirit to see how awkward and shaky I was on my feet. We have some family videos from the 1950's, and it's painful for me to watch myself in those. There is one series of moving pictures from the mid-1950's when I am staggering around, my sister barely touches me, and I fall down. At least I got up again.

Nobody really knew the precise extent of the problem back then, other than issues of "coordination" and "stamina." What I clearly discern now is a weakness in my back and in my left side. The way I compensated back then was to hold my shoulders way back, walking a bit like a tipsy penguin. When I'd get tired, I would kind of hop. Now I realize I did that to avoid falling down when my left leg would otherwise have given way.

My friends didn't make fun of me. That was a great blessing. When I would get tired in walking to school, I'd simply sit down on the sidewalk, rest, and then proceed. If I wasn't feeling well, there were a lot of rests in that "journey" from our home at 793 South Main Street (which now is 723 South Main Street) to Seventh Ward Elementary School (which now is a parking lot).

I do remember a few times at home when it was really bad, and I would have to crawl to get from my bedroom to the bathroom. One reason I have a strong memory of the tile in that bathroom was undoubtedly my proximity to it after crawling back and forth a few times.

I'm not whining, just describing. To prove that, I can tell you what was on the radio one particular time I had that problem. It was the song "The Twist." Before you utter the heretical name "Chubby Checker," the version I was hearing over and over was the <u>original</u> version by Hank Ballard, in 1959! I was 12.

I feel bad for my father Elmer, who I think just couldn't process the fact that his son was kind of gimpy. He had played football for Harrisburg Academy in his high-school days, and was a big, strong guy. He was affectionate toward me, mind you, but was of the school that encouragement/commands to walk straight might have the desired effect. Alas, they didn't.

My mother had also been an athlete. She played on the women's varsity basketball team at Huntingdon High School, in the Class of 1932. She loved hiking, too, and even late in life she was a mainstay of the "Thousand-Hills Hikers" in Huntingdon County, PA.

Back to me. At the suggestion of some friends, Mother once took me for "patterning." It wasn't some ominous mind-control thing, but was an attempt to try to "teach" my muscles to work right by a type of repetitive action. I remember pulling my legs up and down and back and forth over and over in a rather dark second-floor room somewhere in Lewistown. The professionals really tried to help me, but my muscles were not very good students.

Also frustrating my father and my mother was the matter of trousers. I kept falling down and tearing them at the knees. It seemed that I was doing a lot of rolling on the ground at a time when my parents weren't rolling in the dough. After that kept happening, my mother discovered patches, and I became the kid with patches on his pants. It was embarrassing, and I wasn't mature or smart enough to start a sartorial trend by acting as if patches were cool.

My friends at Seventh Ward School were great. They knew I had a problem and really appreciated my efforts to do the physical activities we were called on to do.

In Mr. Gordon Singer's gym class one term, our challenge was to learn the Irish jig, in a number of different step combinations. There were five or six, as I recall. We all persevered in stepping, kicking, and turning until the fateful day when we had to do them all together – a final exam, if you will. At my turn, I launched into my version of the dance, in all its variations, which may well have looked like an extra-terrestrial trying to learn the ways of the human. At the end I got a great round of applause from the other kids. I still remember and appreciate that, over 60 years later.

As I grew older, some of the overt physical manifestations of my problem diminished. In college and law school, I wasn't really hampered that much. Earlier, in secondary school at Mt. Hermon School (now Northfield Mt. Hermon School), the problem had reversed. There the gym teacher couldn't understand that I even <u>had</u> a physical problem because I looked somewhat normal, if uncoordinated.

Well, I really <u>did</u> have a problem. It came out in full bloom on the infamous "Mountain Day." On that day, as a supposed gift to the Seniors, classes were called off and we Seniors would have the "great fun" of climbing Mt. Monadnock in New Hampshire. I, of course, was hoping (I hadn't yet discovered real praying) that it would get cancelled or forgotten. It wasn't. After the bus ride to NH, I struggled up to or near the top, and then had to be carried down by one of the saintly teachers, whose name I have sadly forgotten. Interestingly enough, even though I felt humiliated, nobody commented or criticized, and the teacher acted as if that kind of thing happened every day. God bless them for that.

As I look back on my life, I realize that my physical problems have always been front-and-center. I have to, or feel I have to, address in advance the physical demands or risks of <u>every</u> situation and assess whether I can walk somewhere, climb stairs, have energy, keep up with people, all with anxiety about a possible physical collapse and embarrassment. In giving an account in Heaven before the Lord, would I have to stand or could I sit down ·· even wacky thoughts like that. (On that one, my faith tells me there won't be a problem.)

I realize that my physical issues have made me somewhat solitary, avoiding certain types of group activities. ("What if they want to walk somewhere, and I can't make it?") When I want to exercise, I may take a walk alone, often in the dark with just a flashlight. I usually avoid attending football games. I had a collapse one time at the then Giants Stadium in NJ. My friend Paul Koepff, who was with me, graciously brought his car into the stadium to pick me up.

There <u>were</u> some moments of triumph amidst the physical struggles. I must share one, since it was a favorite of my mother's.

I played on a Seventh Ward Elementary School basketball team. I was on the team probably by designation rather than by anyone's choice. I had a very difficult time shooting with two hands, but, for some reason, I was able to shoot a basketball by throwing it like a baseball with my right hand. It looked weird, but after hours of practice at our garage hoop on South Main Street I actually got kind of good at it.

Our team was having an "away" game at the Buchanan Elementary School on the West side of town. During the game, a lady near my mother commented on the little boy out there who couldn't seem to run or do anything right. My mother drew herself up in righteous indignation and declared, "That is <u>my son</u>!" Man, she was loyal.

Anyway, near the end of the game, someone passed me the ball and I heaved it up from beyond the foul line. It went in, all net! The crowd burst into applause.

Over the years, that game and my performance have passed into McMeen legend. My mother would assert that "Sandy won the game with a shot from half-court!" The truth is that if I hadn't made that shot, we would have lost to Barry Reinard's team 23-4. My thrilling shot brought the score to 23-6. Still, I had my moment on the court. And, hey, if the three-point rule had been in effect, it might have been 23-7!

I tee all this up to give perspective and context to the amazing things the Lord has done for me. He took this gimpy kid and gave him a life as a husband, father, grandfather, corporate lawyer in the cauldron of New York City, then as a touring and recording fingerstyle guitarist, and later as a minister of the gospel of Jesus Christ. Those were miracles. I know. I was there.

3

Double Double, Toil and Trouble

I spent the years 1947 to early June 1960 in Lewistown. Those years have little to do with Macbeth, witches, or brew, as this Chapter title might suggest. But there <u>was</u> some toil, and no small amount of trouble.

My paternal grandparents lived in town, as well as uncles, aunts, and cousins on my father's side. The department store founded by my great-grandfather McMeen (called, you guessed it, McMeen's Store) was there. It was sold in 1957, but I still have a box and ashtrays with the store name on them.

I'll hit the family issues later; kid issues now.

In trying to capture those years under some summary heading, I'm led to report cards from some of my beloved elementary school teachers: Mrs. Vivian Goldberg (1st, 2d and 4th grades) and Mrs. Mary Howell (6th grade). They are revealing. My first term report card in 4th grade contained words from Mrs. Goldberg to the effect of "so happy to have Sandy back in class." The second term report card can be summarized as "having problems with Sandy." I was learning the meaning of the term "deportment," as in "bad deportment."

Mrs. Howell's comments seemed more glowing, paraphrasing: "Sandy has incredible determination." That determination didn't always lead Sandy into good behavior or good directions.

My "deportment" issues actually started before elementary school. I was in Miss Keller's Kindergarten class. I have seen an ancient picture of Miss Keller and our class, and the only thing I remember is the glazed and beleaguered look in Miss Keller's eyes.

The reason I mention Kindergarten is that years later my mother told me that I was the only student in the class who did not receive a grade. It was that pesky "deportment" issue. Miss Keller, the poor thing, didn't quite know what to do with me. Maybe I was "hyper-active" in my gimpiness.

I always seemed to be in trouble, and in great anxiety about being found out. For example, there was the matter of smoking. My friends would accompany me into the woods at the end of Sunset Road, and we would happily and stealthily puff away to our young hearts' delight. Camels tasted SO good. Our parents preferred filtered cigarettes, so we became expert on the smell of Winstons versus Parliaments. There was something cool about 11-year old kids in the woods in rural PA smoking something called "Parliaments." It was rogue and regal at the same time.

I tried inhaling a couple of times, but got coughing so loudly we were in fear of being discovered, apprehended, and incarcerated.

I chuckle even now at our naivete when we discovered what we thought was the perfect venue for our illicit smoking – none other than the ticket office of the high school football field in Lewistown! I wonder if passersby were fooled when they heard giggling inside and saw and smelled smoke issuing from the crevices in that ancient and uninsulated shed.

The fear of apprehension hit a fever pitch one time when I took to smoking one of my father's pipes. He had them lined up in a rack in his den by day of the week. I borrowed Thursday's version one day, took it to the woods with the boys, and promptly lost it. That was a crisis. What would happen when Daddy got home from work?! BAD things. I hurried back to the house, discovered an undifferentiated pile of other pipes, took one and put it in the place where the Thursday pipe had been. Problem solved. He never noticed. Praise God!

"Sandy's determination" led me into some other endeavors that were bad, as in ... destructive. My friend's father owned a radio station, and we had the bright idea one day to take a survey of cars in a local parking lot to see who was tuned to the "right" station. If a car were tuned to the "wrong" station, well, punishment would be inflicted on the poor, unsuspecting antenna of that car. Sadly, a number of cars were tuned to the wrong station. We were found out, punished, and extremely penitent.

Other venues for mayhem existed in Lewistown, including some favorite movie theaters. There, in the dark, we could employ our sawed-off pea-shooters and zap people during the movie. Another favorite juvenile-delinquent activity was lining up cups of soda on the railing of the balcony and knocking them over on unsuspecting patrons below. Yes, we were incredibly annoying.

We also went bowling. I was rather incompetent at that, but worse than that, I didn't <u>look</u> good while bowling. If you look good bowling, that's what's cool; the score is secondary. We went to bowling alleys primarily to play the pinball machines and eat hamburgers.

One time at the Decor Lanes on West 4th Street in Lewistown we were involved in an incident in the men's room. The cherry bomb didn't <u>really</u> damage the toilet, but it made a loud noise, and the proprietor rushed in to confront us. My friend and I were "banned for life" from the Decor Lanes.

Years later, circa 2000 I was in Lewistown to give a guitar concert. My mother was with me for the show, and we drove past the Decor Lanes. It was no longer the <u>Decor</u> Lanes; it was the <u>Lewistown</u> Lanes! Having concluded my 28-year career as a lawyer, I was presented with a legal question, which I shared with my mother: was I banned for <u>my</u> life, or was I banned for the life of <u>Decor Lanes</u>? Since I had outlived Decor Lanes, I could argue that my banishment expired! I would have loved to stop at the place as a 50-something guy and have a good laugh with the owner over the matter, but we were late to the show.

Back to "trouble." We engaged in mayhem on Halloween: messed up people's porches, misappropriated their property, and created general havoc. No rationality was in evidence at all; we were just out of control.

I have two specific memories. I created some mess on a man's porch on Fairview Place, down from the old Black's Hospital in Lewistown, and the man chased me in the dark for blocks, screaming at the top of his lungs. I was terrified, which I believe was his intent, along with inflicting some deserved physical harm on me. Necessity was the mother of invention for the gimp then: I ran for my life!

The second memory was that of being blamed for some destruction of Christmas lights that I did <u>not</u> do. I was outraged that <u>I</u> was accused, never connecting the dots on all the bad things I actually <u>had</u> done in the past. We 11-year-olds can have tunnel vision.

We had some honest fun, like playing ping-pong at my friend Frankie Woods's house. But even that could lead to chaos. When either of us missed a ball, we would be yelling, screaming, and ranting, and take out our frustration with our paddle on the edge of the table. Mrs. Woods was very patient with us, but when the language or din got too intense, she would have to admonish us. After a while the table had a certain sawtooth look at the ends, having been paddled nearly to death. Frankie was always better than I. That didn't help things.

My friends and I would do things like ordering cabs from two cab companies to the same house, and then enjoy the futile arguments that ensued. Gosh, we were obnoxious.

We did have some other honest fun -- riding our bikes around, including a trip from South Hills in Lewistown down to the West End of town on a bypass that was in the process of construction in the late 1950's. That was so great. All downhill. No hands, no helmets, full-speed, massive disasters just waiting to happen. Yet we survived.

The bypass, however, led us to bad thoughts and actions. A friend managed to get his hands on a pellet gun. Since he was 12, it is reasonable for you to conclude that it was not legally purchased. Some ammo was also obtained in the same manner. The legend was that the gun was broken, the friend brazenly took it back to the store to be fixed, and purloined some ammo while the owner was fixing the gun.

Back to the bypass. When the bypass was opened, we thought that it might be a brilliant idea to hide in the trees in South Hills above the road and shoot pellets at the cars proceeding down the bypass. Seriously.

I'll tell you this: we may have been middle-class kids screwing around in central PA, but if we had hit a car, and someone had been injured or killed, there would have been hell to pay. Our youth, penitence, and middle-class status wouldn't have gotten us out of such a hideous mess.

Those incidents are one reason that I connect with prison inmates without viewing them as some kind of different species or type of being. I might well have been an inch away from incarceration for injuring or killing a driver with that gun. If we had been better shots ... well, I don't really want to imagine.

The determination of which Mrs. Howell wrote didn't always lead me into crime. I was driven (OK, "encouraged" by my mother) to enter and often win county book report contests and spelling bees. In my last year for the book-report contest, I was declared a co-winner with classmate Linda Haller. In later years I speculated that Linda probably had the better book report, but I was declared a co-winner based on my earlier efforts.

In 1958 and 1959, I was up at 4 AM each day studying a spelling book whose title I still remember: Six Minutes a Day to Perfect Spelling. I needed a lot more than six minutes, and my spelling wasn't always perfect, but I did win the Mifflin County Spelling Bee in 1958 and 1959. As a 7th grader I went on to win the Junior High School Spelling Bee, up against those big, bad 8th - graders.

It wasn't all glory. In 1960 I suffered the humiliation of going down on the word "squeeze," inexplicably forgetting the "u." I think the Lord was dealing with a pride issue.

What else? In 7th grade, sitting next to a window with the sun blazing through, I was able to demonstrate a scientific principle by setting a crumpled-up yellow paper on fire in magnificent flames with my enormous magnifying glass.

A few notable fights took place in elementary and Junior High school, where I took crazy swings at guys. I apparently wasn't aware of my limitations, to paraphrase Dirty Harry.

I didn't really suffer serious injury, amazingly enough. One time, Stevie Krentzman's mother called mine during lunch to inquire as to my condition after Stevie reported that he had wailed on me. I seemed OK, my mother reported, chalking the incident up to youthful hyperbole. There was also the time when I foolishly whacked a really big, really strong, really mean classmate, and then hid behind the teacher Mrs. Goldberg, as he was trying to get at me. This was in full view and to the great delight of the 4th grade class. I thought he would kill me after school, but he didn't come after me. Sometimes you need to do some whacking, at least against the devil.

I need to cover another matter, if this book is to be anywhere near complete or honest. It involves the type of magazine that contains articles that nobody reads. A friend of mine referred to them back then as "sex books," and they were also quaintly called "girly magazines."

My male friends and I were keenly interested in that literary genre. We managed by illegal means to get our hands on some copies. The immediate problem was where to hide them in one's house so that one's mother wouldn't find them. I was so furtive around one particular hiding place of mine that I can't believe my mother didn't find them. She never did, or at least never admitted it.

One solution, of course, was to focus on the material that we found particularly stimulating, cut it out, and throw the rest of the magazine away. It was easier to hide pages than whole magazines.

A problem arises, however, when one forgets where one has <u>hidden</u> the pages. That problem surfaced on the day we left Lewistown, in early June 1960. My mother, sister, and I were moving to Huntingdon, 35 miles away. More about that later. I remember well the cowboy wallpaper in my room, and the blue bookcases. What I <u>didn't</u> remember was that I had hidden some of my treasures in various places <u>under</u> the bookcases that were being moved. As the movers took the bookcases, some beloved hiding places of mine were revealed. Little folded stacks of pictures were suddenly appearing. Horrified, I looked around to see whether my mother was in the area. Thankfully, she was otherwise occupied. After that close call, I threw the pictures away.

Despite the circumstances under which we moved away from Lewistown, discussed later, it was good for me that I left. The next year I understand that a number of my friends were nabbed in connection with some shoplifting sting. I undoubtedly would have been among them had I stayed.

I learned about "gangs" in Lewistown, the dynamics and the incentives. Ours were pretty innocent. "Johnny Ramsey's Gang" ruled in the elementary school, and basically operated by running amok during recess. Later on, I was part of my neighbor "Stevie Runkle's Gang," where I was unsuccessful in pursuing a higher position in the pecking order. My friends and I swiped a bunch of small American flags from a house that we thought and claimed was "abandoned." The flags were displayed for a time on Stevie's lawn. That achievement was inadequate; I remained Corporal Sandy.

There was also the situation at age 7 or so when, in my mother's words, "Sandy drove the car!" One day I climbed into the car parked in our driveway, loosened the brake, messed with the wheel, and the car drifted backwards perilously close to South Main Street, with some serious traffic whizzing back and forth. The Lord saved me, but the story did ascend over the years to a position in McMeen legend, having received substantial embellishments along the way.

At the house, we had cats, and strange things happened even with them. One cat liked to deposit on the outside mat, as treasures, remains of deceased victims in various grotesque positions. Another cat mysteriously disappeared. My aunt said that it had "gone into the basement." I searched everywhere and couldn't find it. My wife has wisely suggested that it went over the "Rainbow Bridge" on South Main Street, and nobody had the heart to tell me.

There were real girls, of course, in Lewistown, not just pictures in magazines. I was in love with a girl in second grade, but can't remember her name. She may not have known I existed. I was fond of several young ladies, and will refer to them by maiden names: Kaye Stringfellow (who had an identical twin Faye; what a double-blessing for a 3rd grader!). We did homework together at her house on South Main Street. At least, I think that's what we were doing. Linda Deamer and Debbie Passmore were also faves of mine. Linda had beautiful eyes, and Debbie was Queen of the 7th grade dance. Since I was Debbie's date/escort, I concluded that made me King. Debbie told me recently that she had acquired her queenly status by collecting the most pennies, and that the whole thing might have been rigged. No mind; she looked great, and I was King for a Day.

I used to bicycle all the way from the South end of town to the West end just to stare at Debbie's house. If she had stepped outside, I wouldn't have known what to do and might well have had a heart attack right then and there. I was a trouble-maker, but a romantic, too.

4

God and Church in Lewistown

As the preceding indicates, if anyone needed a good dose of the Holy Ghost to straighten him out, it was Sandy. The Lewistown Presbyterian Church on East 3rd Street in Lewistown was a nice brick building, the Rev. William Parsons and his family were wonderful people, the Elmer McMeen family were regular attendees at the church, and Elmer even taught Sunday School. But Sandy was a kid, and he didn't like church.

I was squirmy in church, and had to be disciplined regularly. Mother's most frequent admonition employed the term "self-control," as in the lack thereof. Making things worse was that I had a spirit of the clown on me (and still do). That spirit was not from the Holy Spirit. I do remember climbing out the Sunday school window often, and playing in the cement trough outside the church.

I also remember being at the manse once, where the Parsons lived. There were insects all over the ceiling. It seems that bird food had been left uncovered. Some of God's creatures ate, multiplied, and exercised dominion over the manse. I felt bad for the Parsons, but also made a mental note to keep bird food in covered containers, or else bad things could happen.

There was also the matter of the "Offering Plate Caper." As I sat week by week in church while the offering plates were being passed, I had the bright idea of removing for my personal use an offering envelope some time. I plotted and planned for weeks on how to do it. Sunday came and I was ready. After the service, I passed by the stacked plates and slipped one of the envelopes into my pocket. My heart was beating, and I was flush with my ill-gotten gain.

Where to open it? I couldn't do it there. I had to go home, have lunch (which seemed interminable), and go to my room, close the door, and prepare for riches.

Anticipation being at a fever pitch, I opened the envelope. It contained a dime. One ... thin ... dime. Some family had probably given their kid a dime for the offering plate. As I wrote earlier, God does have a sense of humor. He also taught me a lesson. No more stealing from God's house, or any other house, for that matter. If I had scored a fiver or ten-spot, I might have gotten into a <u>very</u> bad habit. That dime was a lesson from the Lord. I never forgot it.

We can't leave the subject of church without touching on church camp. Some kids really liked camp. I hated it. It wasn't the fault of "Camp Shekinah" or the Godly people who ran it. I, with my physical difficulties, was the problem. Plus being out in the woods really wasn't my thing. I spent innumerable hours making unnecessary pot-holders. Also, I wasn't eager to swim in the pond, occupied by thousands of insects of various sizes and degrees of ferocity. I do remember one year being in love with a cute blond girl from Philipsburg, PA, but that may have been a one-way street.

5

Music in Lewistown

Music has been an incredible blessing in my life. I've sung solo, in a duo, and in choirs, and played various instruments. Listening to music, of course, preceded those endeavors. I need to go way back in my murky past to try to discern sources of the music in my life.

In Lewistown, I always was listening to music, whether on the radio, on records, or live. We would attend concerts at the high school, featuring local groups and those from abroad. I remember that my mother's sister Aunt Anne Pullinger from Bethlehem had something to do with getting the Obernkirchen Children's Choir to perform in Lewistown. We enjoyed that despite my difficulty in pronouncing the group's name.

We had many records at home, and I recall a season of immersing myself in light classical music, including the "Light Cavalry Overture" and the "Poet and Peasant Overture" by Franz von Suppé. Of course, I (and most of the rest of my generation) knew the "William Tell Overture" from the TV series "The Lone Ranger." It was the theme song for that popular show.

I listened to rock and roll on the radio, and was familiar with "Rock Around the Clock." I practically wore out the 45 record of Dave "Baby" Cortez playing the song "The Whistling Organ." His previous and bigger hit was "The

Happy Organ." I ended up bonding with "The <u>Whistling</u> Organ." I discovered decades later that it had something to do with the chord progression.

There is strong evidence that my musical tastes were not super-refined. Our area of central PA got hit big time in 1954 by an evil woman: "Hurricane Hazel." That storm started in the Caribbean and followed the unusual path south to north right through central Kentucky, West Virginia, Maryland, central PA, New York, up into Canada. I remember the scary wind, rain, and racket.

We lost power. Around 3 in the morning, a strange thing happened. Rosemary Clooney's light-hearted rendition of "The Teddy Bears' Picnic" filled the house. It seems I had been listening to that song on a record when the power went out. The power returned, and the record started up right where it had stopped hours before!

I wanted to play trumpet, but I had buck teeth. I was encouraged to take up the clarinet in the 4th grade. Orthodontia came later, with Dr. Eugene Feldman in Lewistown (who, parenthetically, had the earliest and biggest stash of "Peanuts" cartoon books of anyone in the area). Guitar was not a thought in my mind until Senior year of Mt. Hermon School, years later. I also took piano lessons from Mrs. Williamson in town.

I don't remember a lot about clarinet in those days, except enjoying the elementary and Junior High bands, and our concerts where the loyal parents of band members applauded our earnest if less-than-perfect efforts.

One incident I remember all too well was the disastrous time I was part of a quartet of instrumentalists who performed at a recital. I had a solo, and when one of the keys stuck open on my clarinet, I puffed on the horn and no sound came out. None. Deafening silence. The group played on, thankfully, and I received compliments afterwards on my performance. Well, I hadn't made any mistakes, I guess.

I was doing well on piano, as long as I had the assistance of the long piece of paper that sat over the keys and told you what the notes were. When we moved to Huntingdon, the teacher there didn't use that crutch, and my ignorance was exposed. But piano was very useful to my musical knowledge. I learned about key and time signatures, note values, musical symbols, and concepts like crescendo and diminuendo. In guitar workshops years later, I would often use the piano in comparison and contrast with the guitar.

Playing clarinet and piano gave me a perspective on the guitar that allowed me to argue forcefully, and perhaps persuasively, for the greatness of the guitar as an instrument.

I also sang in groups, I'm told, but can't really remember particulars. My mother reminded me once of a concert where I was engaged in some hair-pulling on stage with Miltie Brandt in full view of the audience. She cut me some slack later since she claimed that Miltie started it. Miltie went on to become Mayor of Lewistown, so that incident didn't seem to hurt our careers.

All this is by way of saying that if you expected a musical prodigy, you'll have to go elsewhere.

Jo McMeen at her desk in the mid-1950's.

6

Family

You might be wondering why I haven't discussed my family until now. There are two reasons. First, I didn't want it to appear that my family situation was the cause of my miscreant behavior. The devil and I take responsibility for that. Second, it's difficult for me to write of my family circumstances in the 1950's. I wanted to get a head of steam up first.

We are to honor our mother and father. Even if that weren't a Commandment, we should do it anyway. I had to decide whether or not to include in this book accounts of some rough behavior by my father.

I loved both my parents, and despite what you are going to read here, my father was an affectionate and sociable man who had many friends. He visited our home in New Jersey in later years, hugged our children and us, enjoyed a good meal, football, a good walk, and a good laugh. He wasn't afraid to laugh at himself, either. My sister Franny moved heaven and earth for him as his health declined in the 1990's. She found the perfect apartment for him in Harrisburg, PA, and eventually a spot in a community nursing home there. At his funeral in 1996, the minister at the Harrisburg church recounted his statement to her once that he wasn't the man he <u>wanted</u> to be, but he wasn't the man he <u>used</u> to be, either. At the risk of breaking the flow, I must say this up front.

Back to Lewistown. Let's start with my paternal grandparents in town, Albert Ralph and Elizabeth McMeen. They lived in a substantial stone house overlooking the town. They gave it the name "Ridgewood." I recall it as large and austere (although I didn't know the word "austere" back then). We would have Sunday dinners there frequently.

My grandfather Ralph died at age 67 of a heart attack after a day of work at the store in 1952. I recall him as a friendly man who was nice to me. Grandma McMeen died in 1958.

As to Grandma, I have four recollections. First, she was stern. Second, she berated my mother for having my blond hair cut into a crewcut, fashionable at that time. (She may have been right on that, since my time for hirsuteness was to be sadly limited.) Third, I remember this famous conversation with Grandma one Thanksgiving:

Grandma: "Sandy, do you want white meat or dark meat?"
Sandy: "White meat, Grandma."
Grandma: "Well, you'll take some of each."

Finally, there was the time one Sunday when Grandma made me an inedible grilled-cheese sandwich. I don't know whose idea it was, but my sister Franny and I repaired to the bathroom and proceeded to flush it down the toilet piece-by-piece, while successfully avoiding detection despite laughing through the risky thrill of it all.

My father's brother Hugh and his wife Grace lived in town, along with Uncle Albert and Aunt Margie McMeen,

Uncle Fred and Aunt Jane Fiigon, and assorted beloved cousins. Uncle Albert and Aunt Jane were my father's brother and sister. Along with what I will recount later, there was a lot of family sadness in or relating to Lewistown. We lost Aunt Margie, Aunt Jane and years later Aunt Grace to cancer, along with my father's other sister Sarah. Aunt Sarah was married to Uncle Ed Mancke and lived with her family in Bethlehem, PA.

Now to the group at 793 South Main Street. Residing at our house were Elmer, Josephine, Franny, Sandy, and one or more cats. Two other residents were there: Alcohol and Tension. Alcohol lived for free, since we all paid the price for it.

My sister Franny was 4-1/2 years older than I. As we all know, that might as well be 100 years when you're 13. She was finishing up Lewistown High School and I was 13, getting into trouble.

Franny was smart and did some really impressive things that I personally witnessed. She was selected by the American Field Service for a summer abroad in Finland. When she returned, she gave a number of speeches in the area about her experience, and they were <u>great</u>! She was amusing and informative, with entertaining visual aids decades before PowerPoint.

Franny went on to Ursinus College for a year, then transferred to Penn State, Main Campus. She earned her Master's in Library Science from Pitt, ending up in New York City, where she seemed to live forever on the Upper West Side. After a few years, her address rolled off the tongue: "788ColumbusAvenueApartment10S." She had jobs in various libraries and other organizations, including the Theresa M. Burke Employment Agency and Goldman Sachs.

She also was a devotee of the books of Barbara Pym, an English novelist who died in 1980. Franny was a loyalist in the Barbara Pym Society, North America, along with many dear friends. Those included Beverly Bell and Barbara Dunlap, who gave generous and loving help to her when she was fighting cancer.

Franny was really funny. She could have been a stand-up comedian I'm convinced. One time, Franny was explaining in detail to my mother and me her protocol with respect to the timeliness of blind dates. If a blind date were 15 minutes late, then Franny would leave the assigned location. She went on to discuss the fact that, despite that, she had allowed a particular blind date 30 minutes to arrive. We inquired why. She answered that her protocol afforded an extra 15 minutes for blind dates who were actually blind. It seems she had met a gentleman at Lighthouse for the Blind in New York City and had to adjust her protocol. The way she told this left us in stitches.

On September 11, 2001, there was a period of eight hours when I didn't know whether Franny had survived the 9/11 attacks in New York City. Her routine was to go through the World Trade Center at almost precisely the time of the attacks, on her way to Goldman Sachs. When I ultimately reached her, praise God, it turns out that she had gone to vote in midtown Manhattan in the primary election that took place that day. She hadn't been downtown at all. Sadly, Franny died of cancer at age 62 in 2005. God was around even that situation as I will share later.

Back to the residents of 793 South Main Street. My parents' generation seemed to drink a lot. Some of that activity no doubt was a response to WW II, but some pre-dated it. My father had drinking problems on my parents' honeymoon, my mother told me. That was ominous. He was unhappy, perhaps with the family store, perhaps in the town, perhaps with family responsibilities. I can say the last one because in later years my father lived by himself in a walk-up room in Harrisburg, PA, and said more than once that he was at heart a "hermit."

I have seen pictures of my mother as a college student, whimsical and happy, and then pictures of her from the 1950's, and the change is striking. A cloud had descended on her countenance in many of those pictures. Not all; she had many happy moments with family, garden-club, hospital, church, and other activities. But many.

Martinis were the usual offender. Pitchers of martinis. Even at this stage of my life, I can barely comprehend the concept of a <u>pitcher</u> of martinis for one person. Some people get happy when they drink. My father didn't. Things got dark. If he was drinking and listening to music, for example, and my mother asked him to turn the music down, he would turn it all the way up. Things like that, and worse.

Mother would prepare dinner and he wouldn't show up. I would often be delegated the task of calling Daddy at the Lewistown Elks Club and imploring him to come home for dinner. Sometimes he would, but not timely. When he would be at dinner, the conversation would often be strained and accusatory, with my father patronizing my mother and she, in turn, threatening to throw a glass of water at him. One time she did, and I thought all hell would break loose. My father just laughed. Maybe he knew he was out of line.

I wasn't allowed to cross South Main Street. I would beg my father to go to Bachmann's Store, right across the street, and get me some baseball cards. As an aside, I was constantly hoping for another Mickey Mantle card. Instead, I always seemed to get the card of someone named "Roman Mejias." If you don't know who he was, search his name on the Internet. He did play in The Bigs, but definitely <u>wasn't</u> "The Mick."

Bachmann's was a one-minute walk away. Daddy would go for baseball cards, and 45 minutes later would return, having taken the route down the street, through the bar at the Green Gables Hotel, and back. That happened more than once.

We would go out to restaurants, and Daddy would drink, and play the pinball machines. Sometimes I would play, too. After several drinks, the pinball games would become more difficult, and enraging, and there might be a scene. These are not pleasant memories, but I can't leave them out.

There were some really bad scenes. I had repressed this one for years. After drinks one night, my father got enraged at my sister for some reason, took a pair of scissors, and whacked off her hair as she was screaming in fear and horror. I can't imagine what that did to the psyche of a teenage girl.

One Valentine's Day, in the late 1950's, my father had a car accident, staggered into our house, and collapsed, bloodied and smelling of alcohol. I was terrified and remember asking, "Mother, is he dead?" He had wrecked the second new car in a week. He recovered, but I remember those next few days when he sat in his den, staring out the window.

My mother consulted her minister, the Lord, Scripture, and her sisters and friends. She didn't want to give up, and divorce back then left a stigma.

There were too many incidents for me to know the tipping point, and I was just a kid, but I do remember one situation that might have qualified. On Easter (of all days), after church my mother made some comment to Daddy about his mother, and Daddy hauled off and slapped her, right in front of us kids. We were screaming and bawling, but Mother was tough. She didn't cry.

In early June 1960, I waved to my father out the window of my mother's car, as Mother, Franny, and I left Lewistown and moved 35 miles away to the town of Huntingdon, PA.

View from Flagpole Hill, Huntingdon, PA.

7

Spiritual Intermission I

Let's take a breather, and ask: *where was God in all this?*

I don't know where my sister was spiritually back then. As for me, I'm the kid who had the bright idea of swiping from the offering plate, so my theology wasn't exactly pristine. My father had read the Bible straight through, and taught Sunday school, but was having problems applying in real life the teachings and model of Jesus through the power of the Holy Spirit.

My mother and her line, however, are very interesting. Her parents died in 1936, eleven years before I was born. Oh, I wish I had known them. From looking at pictures, I have the impression that Grandma Biddle cracked the whip back then. I have found some support for that in letters, and tales from my mother and aunts. I can't imagine what it was like for my mother at age 22 to lose both parents in the same year. Grandma Biddle died of cancer and Grandpa of a heart attack – or as my mother said, a broken heart after his wife died.

Grandpa Biddle trained as a lawyer at Dickinson Law School. When I arrived at Penn Law School in 1969, I pawed through ancient tomes in the library and discovered to my pleasure that Grandpa Biddle had been on the Law Journal at Dickinson, an honor that both my wife Sheila and I would later have at Penn. He left the law, however, having gotten the journalism bug, and founded, among other newspapers, the Huntingdon PA Daily News.

Mother was one of five children, and was born in Everett, PA in 1914. She was significantly younger than the others, and was blond and frisky. Her brother, my Uncle John Biddle, liked to tell her she was adopted because she looked different from the others. Subsequently, the family moved to Huntingdon. Mother attended public schools there, from William Smith Elementary School through Huntingdon High School.

In regard to Mother and her mother Anna Hunter Biddle, I am reminded of the story of Timothy in the Bible. Timothy was the young pastor mentee of the apostle Paul. He became leader of the church at Ephesus. Timothy's strong faith derived from his mother's line, his grandmother Lois and his mother Eunice. That really hit me, because that's my case, too.

My Grandmother Biddle grew up in Philadelphia, and was a real evangelist for the Lord. I ran across the following inscription in a Bible presented to her in 1889 by her then minister. It read as follows:

"This book is presented to Annie Hunter as a reward for bringing a larger number of new members into her Band than any other individual Band member. The prayer of the giver is that she may ever bring many to the work of Christ, and more to the blessed Christ himself."

It was dated May 14, 1889, and signed "Your affectionate pastor, Willie B. Skillman."

Grandma was 13 years old at the time, and that "Band" was probably part of the Salvation Army Band, or a comparable church organization.

As for my mother, I've seen evidence that her favorite verses (in earlier translations, of course) included Micah 6:8:

"He has shown you, O man, what *is* good;
And what does the Lord require of you
But to do justly,
To love mercy,
And to walk humbly with your God?"

She also made mention of Psalm 46:10:

"Be still, and know that I *am* God;
I will be exalted among the nations,
I will be exalted in the earth!"

I don't know the depth of Mother's revelation on the gospel, or her faith that the supernatural power of God could take seemingly intractable situations like Elmer and Josephine and fix them. My suspicion is that she didn't think in those terms, but instead sought wisdom and counsel on whether she should stay with Elmer or not.

As for me in sharing these matters somewhat dispassionately, I have sought guidance from the Lord. I need to make sure that this Lewistown experience didn't leave me with such scar tissue that I become insensitive to difficult situations affecting other people. Romans 12:15 calls on us to weep with those who weep. Sometimes I am so concerned to avoid "enabling" a person into "victimhood" that I turn too quickly to "fixing" rather than "weeping" mode. "Fix with those who weep" doesn't appear in the Bible.

All of us need to be branches on the vine of Jesus, tenderized in that area where we connect with the Lord, without hardness like unbelief, anger, or unforgiveness building up there. I don't want to wallow in past hurt and sadness, but I don't want to ignore them either. Jesus in His earthly ministry was, among other things, a "man of sorrows," who endured temptation and pain, and as our high priest understands the burdens we bear.

8

Huntingdon, PA

Our dear Lewistown friend Mary Boyer helped us in our move to Huntingdon in June 1960. It was she who uttered the words now famous in McMeen lore: "Mrs. McMeen, you've got five feet of water in your basement!" With that sentence, we received our welcome to 1317 Moore Street, Huntingdon, PA. A contractor eventually pumped the water out. (In the late 1970's my mother moved to Shadyside Avenue, near the high school. She said Moore Street had gotten too noisy.)

1317 Moore was a nice, blue, two-story house on a street that by its name might sound like a quiet residential way. It wasn't. It was a main thoroughfare in town. I guess Mother felt that Sandy wouldn't be "driving the car" perpendicularly into the street. The car would be parked on the street, parallel to the sidewalk, or safely at the rear of the property.

Huntingdon was a smaller town than Lewistown, and seemed more connected to its rural roots than Lewistown was. Both were county seats, but there was a more intimate feel to Huntingdon, with a smaller downtown and more immediate views of the surrounding hills. The predominant industry in Huntingdon County was agriculture. (In Lewistown I had never been aware of the proximity of the hills, except perhaps South Hills and dealing with the good, old bypass.)

While Lewistown was bigger, and had more industry at the time, Huntingdon had two institutions that were to outlive much of the industry in Lewistown. One was a fine liberal-arts college, Juniata College, which was right up Moore Street from our house. The other was referred to affectionately (though not by the residents thereof) as "SCI." SCI was the State Correctional Institution at Huntingdon. Another prison, "SCI-Smithfield," was built later, in 1988, right up the hill from SCI. The college and the prisons, in their different ways, were and are a blessing to Huntingdon, providing employment and resources for many people in town (and in the case of at least one of my Lewistown classmates, SCI provided room and board).

In my personal life, Huntingdon is a bit of an anomaly. It is in a sense a "co-hometown" with Lewistown. Yet it was an escape from the turmoil of our life in Lewistown. It was also the place where I made my first mature decision: to be a "good boy" and not do anything to embarrass my mother. I remember the day I made that decision. On that front, I had substantial, if not complete, success.

Huntingdon is a town that when I go through the names of the members of my high school class, I can still remember a vast number of them. I have fond memories of them, to boot. It is a town in which my wife and I were married in 1971 and to which we were to return in 2012 to live for five years. It is a town with which our family, including my father, was connected even while we lived in Lewistown. We would visit our Biddle relatives there often, at their cottage on Lake Raystown, and the big, old, fascinating house near the top of 5th Street Hill, with its wood/coal-burning furnace and spooky third floor. (Mother loved that house, and told us many stories of growing up there.)

Yet, it also was a town in which I lived for basically three years, before going off for 11th and 12th grades to Mt. Hermon School in 1963. Once you go away to a boarding school, you are gone, at least in an emotional sense. One of your roots is pulled up, or at the very least, becomes attenuated.

In June of 1960, however, the most salient fact for us was that Huntingdon contained two institutions in which my mother and her family had an ownership interest, and where she had paying jobs: the Huntingdon Daily News and Radio Station WHUN. Thank God for them. They supported our family, and provided funds for my sister's and my college education and my two years at Mt. Hermon.

The family situation had changed radically: my sister was on her way off to college, Ursinus and then Penn State, and the day-to-day household became my mother and me, and she was working a lot.

Mother was very direct with us when we moved: "Now I have to be mother and father to you kids." I heard and could understand that as an early teenager, but it had a deeper significance that I grasped only decades later. Many men have warm-and-fuzzy memories of their mothers; my memories dating from the Huntingdon period were of a woman who was loving, but aggressive, effective, and busy. She initiated and pursued causes, created organizations, sat on Boards, covered all kinds of events for the newspaper, had a twice-weekly newspaper column, had a daily radio program and a weekly program, and worked into her late 80's. She loved the area, knew a bunch of people, and even more people knew her or knew of her. Jo McMeen was a force.

In June 1960 Jo McMeen must have been more of an emotional mess than a force, but she didn't let on. It did feel weird to me, however, with just the two of us in the house. But I didn't miss Alcohol and Tension, who had resided with us in Lewistown.

9

Getting Along

I missed my Lewistown friends, especially the co-laborers in my various acts of delinquency. But I had made my declaration to try to be good. That required me to move forward and not gaze for too long in the rear-view mirror.

I got to know the two neighbor kids, one on each side of the house. The first was Charlie Hoffman. What an All-American name, I thought! No "Elmer Ellsworth McMeen, III." No name that would embarrass you when called out in elementary school. Charlie was a year ahead of me in school, and a good guy.

Next, I met the Hess's on the other side of the house. Kenny was in my class, and his younger sister was Karen. Mr. Hess worked at SCI. Kenny and I got really close, and still correspond, nearly 60 years later. He specialized in the sciences that I avoided in college like the plague. His mother Katie lived to be over 100.

The good thing for me education-wise in Huntingdon was that 8th grade combined students who had earlier gone to separate schools. I wasn't the only outsider; in a sense, everyone was an outsider. I didn't feel isolated as the out-of-towner. 8th grade at the Junior High School was a new scene for everyone. That may have been a "God-thing," arranging the chess pieces that way, or maybe Mother had scoped all that out in advance. Mother was sharp, but she had a <u>lot</u> of stuff on her mind in early 1960, and the demographics of 8th grade in Huntingdon probably weren't among them.

The Junior High School was a few blocks down on Moore Street. It used to be the old high school my mother had attended back in the day.

I don't remember much about 8th grade. It's all a bit hazy. I do recall that Mr. Ralph Weaver, a very good teacher, had some sinus problem that obliged him periodically to open the window during class and expectorate out the same. That was different, and gave an interesting rhythm to the class. It may be legend, but I <u>think</u> I recall that his sputum once hit another teacher on the head. He apologized, presented her with a nice bouquet of flowers, and all was well.

I also remember the coldest day I've ever experienced, in early 1961. I walked to school in minus 16 degrees, with a howling wind and before the time when wind chill was invented to make us feel even worse. I didn't whine and beg my mother to drive me, but I <u>should</u> have. I was kind of clueless back then.

I continued to have the occasional altercation with larger, stronger individuals in the area. Sam Weidel lived in the neighborhood, and my existence rubbed him the wrong way. He wore a constant scowl when I was around. Some pushing and shoving escalated into a brawl when he tilted the pinball machine I was playing right when I was ready to rack up a free game. In our world, that was a capital offense. We were in a small store, so we didn't have much room to take big swings, which probably saved me. I don't know whatever happened to Sam. Maybe he's writing his own book about redemption.

In the area of music, I still played clarinet (and would get quite serious about it in high school). Our Junior High band leader was Mr. Ted Yoder, a fine gentleman, and patient. I later took lessons with Mr. Brownagle. He could play trumpet <u>and</u> clarinet (which placed him high in the musical pantheon to me). He blew my mind once by doing a glissando up <u>and then down</u> on the clarinet. (As to what a glissando is, think of the beginning of "Rhapsody in Blue.") I could kind of fake my way through the ascending glissando, but to do both made him god-like to me. His place was a little dark, and had a vague aura of must and smoke, making the lesson experience even cooler.

Mother set me up for piano lessons with Mrs. Swan, a pleasant and well-meaning lady, just a block from our house. Her son Robert was ahead of me in school, was a great trumpet player, and an even better pianist. He would go on to make a name for himself in music out on the West Coast. I on the other hand didn't practice enough, invented lame excuses for missing lessons, and was otherwise a D piano student.

A rolled-up newspaper, "posed" to set
up the next chapter.

10

My Career in Media: Paperboy

My life of indolence was not to last in Huntingdon. Without formal application, I was hired for my second job in Media. I became a paperboy. (In Lewistown I had made good money delivering "TV Guides" in the South end of town.) I was to deliver copies of the Daily News to nearly 100 people in Huntingdon. It was a serious responsibility for a kid, to be sure, but not that rare. I spoke about it with people in later years. It seems that almost everyone at one time or another had delivered papers for the Daily News.

My route was not the best route, of course, I being a newbie. It <u>was</u> convenient. After school I would go downtown and hang out near the back of the plant. If there were time, I would shoot a little pinball in Skeetz's store next door, and shoot the breeze with a lovable character there, Charlie Morningstar.

Inside the newspaper building the press would be roaring and two muscular men, Al Jamison and Harold Everhart, would be working the machinery. The Circulation Manager collected and distributed the papers. The offices, including my mother's, were in the front then. This was all before photo-offset technology rocked the printing world.

I'd pick up my papers and start up Washington Street from 4th Street, where the radio station was. There weren't a lot of papers to deliver for blocks, so lots of bike-riding but not much tossing of folded papers until 9th Street. Things really picked up at 10th street, and the part from 11th to the end of my route at 13th street was a cornucopia of customers. At 13th and Washington, I was only two blocks from home.

I'm glad I stayed well during that period because nobody really could have covered for me. Some people got their papers in the door, some on the porch, some in the back, and in the case of one nice lady, up the back stairs and into her living room. (Her grandson years later thanked me for delivering her paper to her up the back stairs!)

I didn't know at the time that I was a little "commission merchant." What I was doing was, in essence, buying the papers from the company with the aggregate weekly amount that I was allowed to keep. If the paper were 35 cents a week, and I got to keep a nickel per customer, I had to be sure that I collected enough to pay for <u>all</u> the papers at 30 cents per paper per week. That was the leverage the company had over the paperboys, and it was proper. Nobody complained. It was all settled each week when we paperboys brought in our bags full of pennies, nickels, and whatever. Annie Miller would then proceed to work her magic and count money faster than any other human, before or since.

I figured out that customers who paid yearly didn't really help me much, unless they were generous toward me at Christmas. (Some were, mercifully.) People who paid monthly in arrears meant that I might have a cash flow situation pending their payment. In general, I really needed for people to pay in a timely manner or I had a problem.

One situation came to a head. A woman, let's call her Mrs. X, seemed to disappear when I came to collect. It happened all the time. I'd approach, and a shadowy figure inside would head to the back. After this kept happening, I left a little note in her door with the plaintive question: "Mrs. X, why do you always hide when I come to collect?" Those might not have been the exact words. Whatever they were, she got furious and charged down to the newspaper office to complain. I don't know exactly what happened. Maybe apologies were issued with the promise to "talk to Sandy" about it. My suspicion is that the powers-that-be, namely, my Uncle John Biddle (the publisher), my aunts, and my mother, got a kick out of it. They probably didn't think too highly of a doctor's wife trying to stiff the paperboy.

Then there was the "Great Paperboy Contest." The paper held a contest to see which paperboy could get the most new subscribers. The prize was one's choice of a weekend trip to New York City, or $50 cash. When Uncle John announced the contest, my mother approached him and asked, "What are we going to do when Sandy wins the contest?" Uncle John seemed surprised. "Why do you think Sandy will win the contest?" "He just will," was her response.

You can guess what happened. I don't remember what I did, but I must have engaged in begging, pleading, pathetic looks, or something, because I got 10 or 15 new subscribers along a route that was considered if not the Land of Nod, nevertheless not the Garden of Eden. I took the $50, and Mother let me squander some of it.

I remember well the article in the paper, together with the picture of the kids who chose to go to New York with the Circulation Manager. <u>They</u> looked very excited; the look on <u>his</u> face seemed to me, even in my youth, as something akin to resignation with a dash of dread.

11

High School

After my wife Sheila and I returned to Huntingdon in 2012, I found myself being drawn to the high school. Part of the reason was that there were whole streets, and scores of houses, that didn't exist in 1961. I would drive up and down Murray Avenue, Cassady Avenue, and Brumbaugh Avenue trying to visualize the way things had been 50 years earlier. I also took note of some ranch houses that I had hoped would have been for sale when we were buying, but weren't.

But it was more than that. There was something about the high school. I was like the kids who hang around the school in summer. What's with that? All school year they're in the building, and when summer comes, all they want to do is ride their bikes in the school parking lot.

The reason, for those kids and this kid, is, of course, that unlike the situation during the school year, in summer you could come and go as _you_ pleased. You'd go there at _your_ pleasure, and leave the same way. It was all about freedom.

I spent two school years at Huntingdon Area High School ("HAHS"), 1961-1963. The building was a garden-variety, sprawling PA high school, but relatively new and well-lighted. Our class was quite large, over 300 kids as I recall. The scene was quite different from the ancient Junior High School, not only in the physical surroundings but also in the fact that we went from top of the student demographic heap to the bottom in the space of a short summer. We were Freshmen in a world of big, strong, older people who might toy with and torment us.

It turned out not to be so bad. We were mostly ignored by the older students, with some minor mocking and admonitions. There was no hazing, just a lot of hurried walking up and down long halls to get to class on time.

I remember some rather descriptive, if not the most complimentary, names for certain teachers there. Mr. J. Allen Isett, who taught Biology, was referred to as "Bugsy." That seemed appropriate, due not only to the subject matter, but also to the fact that when he got excited, his eyes seemed to bug out a bit. Then there was Mr. John Rittenhouse, who taught math. He was referred to as "Corpsey," a rather unkind reference to his pallor. Mr. Rittenhouse apparently spent more time with math books than sunning himself on the beach in Atlantic City.

We didn't have a nickname for the gym teacher, Mr. Elwood Reese. We didn't want to mess with him. He was in great shape and had a certain stern hauteur that was a little scary. He was always "Mr. Reese." More about him later.

The most terrifying of the teachers was Mrs. Blanche Z. Scholey. She taught 9th grade English and hectored even some of her fellow teachers, I found out later. She was a very attractive older lady. She had won beauty contests at Juniata College back in the day, my mother told me. She had beautiful, if cold, blue eyes, a steely demeanor, and grammar perfectionism in her heart. She also had tremendous energy, handing out papers, taking them back, rushing around the room, and beating grammatical rules into our brains that still rattle around in there. ("Objective case before an infinitive!") She brooked no nonsense.

To prove her influence: years later I did a guest article for the Daily News. My mother, an English major at Cornell, committed a rare and unthinkable atrocity on my piece. She took a perfectly innocent sentence and turned it into one with a grotesquely dangling participle. I berated her, saying, "Mrs. Scholey is going to see that!" Mrs. Scholey really got into our heads.

I remember my home room teacher one year, Mr. Angelo Ciarrocca. He was new. He got tired of some constant sass from a classmate of mine, charged his chair, knocked the chair over with my classmate in it, and threatened some mayhem on his body. Even we were shocked.

I did well in high school academically, although there were times when girls I was dating did better. I'd get a 94, and Dorrie Miller would get a 95; I'd get a 95 and Nancy Snare would get a 96. Grrrr. I was competitive.

Mr. Harvey McElhoes taught the "World Cultures" course. It was the first time he taught it. He was honest enough to say that he was staying three pages ahead of us in the textbook. He was so enthusiastic about the subject matter ("Hey, this stuff is <u>interesting</u>!"), that he could absolutely be forgiven.

Mr. McElhoes also taught Driver Ed. Part of the McMeen lore is his statement to me one time while I was driving, or attempting to drive: "McMeen, I know you're smart, but you're a <u>dumb</u> driver!" I do like alliteration.

I usually was in agita during the class occurring right before gym class. I would be speculating about what the particulars of my upcoming embarrassment would be that day. The worst gym days were when we did exercises and activities with the girls. My incompetence would be in full view of people I might be dating, or wanted to be. Nobody would be paying attention to me, probably, but when you're not doing well, you feel all eyes are upon you.

The school administration was aware that I had issues with gym. My mother had seen to that. She was afraid that my inadequacies in gym class would lead to a grade keeping me off Honor Roll and hurt my chances of getting into a good college. In fact, the principal Norman Smith was considering something like that.

Back to gym. It was demanding. On a nice, sunny day Mr. Reese would lead the pack of us in a run to the Juniata College fields. That was just for starters. We would then run around and play soccer or something, or do exercises, and then run back. Gimpy Sandy struggled with all that.

Then in 1962 or thereabouts, there was the impending horror of the "President's 600-Yard Run." President Kennedy declared that high school students should become more fit, and established a 600-yard run as a requirement. My pleas to God for rain on gym class days were met quite a few times, but eventually they weren't.

The day for the run was a gorgeous Spring day. Oblivious to the idea of pacing myself, I charged ahead of the pack for a distance of 40 yards. Then things got tough. We were to run up the road 300 yards toward the college, and then return. To my amazement, I did not finish last. I was next-to-last. The classmate who had that distinction, however, also had a good excuse: he was really sick that day.

Things came to a head regarding gym class. While attempting a back somersault on the mat, I broke my left-hand thumb. It swelled up to the size of a lemon. My mother reported to me, with some amusement, that when the school administration heard that I had busted a bone in gym class, someone exclaimed, "Oh, no, not the McMeen boy!" I don't think they were eager to engage in a further discussion with Mother about Sandy and gym class.

I had a "sports-related injury." That was kind of cool. Even better, I got yanked out of gym class and had an extra study hall. But my injury really messed up my clarinet practice for District Band. Which brings us to the subject of music.

This reminded me of a row of musicians at District Band.
See next chapter.

12

Music in Huntingdon

An outsider might look at Huntingdon as some kind of sleepy little town tucked away in the hills and farmland of America. Even my sister, steeped in her supposedly sophisticated years in Manhattan, would occasionally refer to Huntingdon as "the town that time forgot." She wasn't really that serious, but quoting some movie, I think. In fact, Franny loved to visit Huntingdon and attend with my mother the Huntingdon County Fair, "Hartslog Valley Day," and the periodic shows at the McConnellstown Playhouse.

One passion in Huntingdon was music. Huntingdon turned out many fine musicians. The high school and college put on performances, both choral and instrumental, that were excellent by any reasonable standard. High school kids routinely made Regional and State band and chorus, and sometimes even All-Eastern US band and chorus. Some would go on to join the illustrious Penn State Blue Band, or become teachers and performers.

I was starting to have my moments on clarinet. I worked for hours, days, and weeks to learn by ear all or most of the clarinet solo in the song "High Society," played by Kenny Ball and His Jazzmen. I was taking lessons from one of the best musicians to come out of Huntingdon, Natalie Laird Ozeas. I always had stamina problems playing clarinet. Natalie tried to help me, but I think they stemmed from the

59

CP. I didn't want to admit that at the time, because it wasn't solvable.

I was doing well in band in 10th grade, in the first clarinet section behind our first chair Andy Schmitt, the very attractive Elaine Russell, and some other upperclassmen. Mr. Lester Garman was our leader. I did tend to cut up during band practice a bit with my friend Bruce Kauffman, mocking some of the less competent or less serious musicians among us, but at least I wasn't shooting at cars anymore. Bruce played tuba (and sang) and would eventually make it all the way to Regional Band and All-State Chorus (and later a Ph.D. from the University of Chicago). Sharon Grubb made it to All-Eastern US Band after I left, an achievement beyond my wildest dreams.

My greatest musical achievement in Huntingdon went relatively unnoticed, to my great disappointment for many years. It turned out, however, to be a training ground for me, through a miracle of God. In a period of under three weeks in 2005 I wrote a book of arrangements of traditional Celtic pieces for classical string trio (violin, viola, and cello, three instruments I didn't play). The book is called Celtic Treasures for String Trio.

What happened back in the 1960's was this: I became smitten with the Elmer Bernstein song "Walk on the Wild Side," as played by the Si Zentner band. It had some tricky syncopation and a bluesy quality. I loved that song. I played it over and over. In a burst of enthusiasm, I decided to arrange it for our high school band. I spent weeks figuring out the keys for the various instruments, and writing the whole thing out for band instruments. When I was finished,

I presented my work to Mr. Garman. He looked puzzled at all the handwritten music, but said we'd try it.

What happened was that the band couldn't seem to get into the music. I played the record so that people could hear the tune. It was just not meant to be. Mr. Garman had other music he had prepared for us, apparently, and nobody appreciated the monumental effort it took for a 10th grade kid to do what I had done. I'm not blaming anyone, but I am putting it out there this way, keeping it real. The handwritten music is lost. I may have thrown it all away in my discouragement.

God remembered that whole episode and blessed me 40 years later with my Celtic strings book. And He did it at the perfect time for my soul, during the heartbreaking period in 2005 when my sister was succumbing to cancer. Later on, we will get to the other thing He did in that period.

Back to band. I was selected for District Band in 1963. That was pretty heady for a Sophomore. I was all set to launch into a massive practice campaign when I broke my thumb in gym. I was sidelined for six weeks, unable to practice. I had a couple weeks to prepare after the cast came off, but it wasn't the same. I placed 6th in second clarinet out of thirteen. Another major disappointment.

The concert took place in Clearfield, PA, during a snowstorm. My mother drove up for the show, but we had to stay in a motel and return the next day.

I did enjoy getting to know a great sax player from Dubois, PA, Dorothy Mikelonis. Her older sister Marianne was a clarinet goddess to me, having won first chair, first clarinet at District. Dorothy was also a great musician, and went on to become Valedictorian of her class in high school. She probably doesn't remember me, but I remember her and her sister.

I was also doing some singing back then, but can't remember many details. I wasn't in any of the high school singing groups, but have a vague recollection of singing in the choir at the Lutheran Church in Huntingdon and receiving a compliment or two from fellow choir members.

Which leads us to church.

13

God and Church in Huntingdon

The still, small voice of the Lord kept me out of serious trouble in Huntingdon. He didn't break my thumb; He didn't do wrong by failing to keep the rain away to spare me the "President's 600-Yard Run;" He didn't place me in 6th chair, second clarinet, at District Band.

I did fail Him once, however, in an act of weakness. I "borrowed" a magazine from the rack at a store in Huntingdon and forgot to "return" it. That's the most charitable way of putting it. Years later, I did partial penance; I sent $20 to the store, figuring the double-sawbuck reflected a serious inflation adjustment for the 25-cent magazine I had pilfered 40 years earlier. I chickened out, however, and didn't give my name, so my attempt for absolution was miserably inadequate.

On the other hand, I may have won a soul for Jesus. The store had changed hands a few times in the interim, and the person receiving the $20 bill in the envelope may well have thought that the Lord, in His grace, dropped a twenty on him from Heaven (albeit via the State of New Jersey, according to the postmark).

So where was God in that, you may properly ask? Well, my mother found the magazine in our house. I had been negligent in hiding it. She decided to make an object lesson out of it. I wasn't to be rebuked or admonished, but educated. So, my mother provided me with books of all kinds of fine art displaying the female body in all its pulchritude, although in some cases lacking limbs and looking a little, well, cold.

Mother was really proud of that endeavor, and referred to it several times in later years. I didn't have the heart to tell her, "Mother, it's really <u>not</u> the same thing."

Moving from sin to church. We attended the Lutheran Church in Huntingdon, and sat in the "family row" up front. Mother was very serious about her faith and the church, and, in fact, was the first woman ever elected to the Board of the Lutheran Theological Seminary in Gettysburg, PA. She was prayerful, and sang the liturgy each week with the congregation. I was still a kid, and got weary of the rote singing, and also standing up so much in the Lutheran Church. (When Mother moved to the Presbyterian Church later in her life, there was less liturgy and less standing.) Church itself was still not having an impact on me.

Something powerful did, however, happen to me around that time. It was the first serious revelation of something in the spiritual realm I had ever received. I reacted to it by making the "wrong" decision, but God takes the long view sometimes – maybe all the time; I don't know.

Before getting into it, I need the right vocabulary to explain it. I didn't receive that until nearly sixty years later. I am so grateful that the Lord led me to a concept that allowed many things to fall into place. He has a way of doing that, and by interesting means.

We'll start with the negative: what happened to me was not a "born-again experience," nor was it a "baptism in the Holy Spirit." It was something else that I couldn't put my finger on until I read a great book by Os Guinness, called Fool's Talk: Recovering the Art of Christian Persuasion (InterVarsity, 2015). On page 134 of that book, Dr. Guinness references the book by Professor Peter L. Berger entitled A Rumor of Angels (Doubleday Anchor, 1970), and Berger's term "signals of transcendence." (Ibid, p. 53)

Berger defines that term as "phenomena that are to be found within the domain of our 'natural' reality but that appear to point beyond that reality." (Ibid) Such a signal does not lead the person inevitably to Christ; it might or might not.

Guinness puts it this way (Fool's Talk, p. 134):

"Such experiences beep like a signal, impelling us to transcend our present awareness and think more deeply, widely and seriously. The signal's message is a double one: it acts as a contradiction and a desire. It acts as a contradiction in that it punctures the adequacy of what we once believed. And it arouses in us a desire or longing for a new answer that is surer, richer and more adequate than whatever it was we believed before--which has patently failed."

I have found that term incredibly useful in assessing my spiritual life. It doesn't quite fit what I'm going to recount here, but it's close.

At some point during the Huntingdon period -- or the first Huntingdon period, I should say -- I got a revelation of the vastness and depth of God and the universe, and the extraordinary sweep and power of the divine through time and space. It was overwhelming. But there was a further "word." If I were to reflect on the grandeur of all that, I would be "immobilized." That is the exact word that came to me. If you put down this book, and reflect on that statement, its power may well come to you, if it hasn't already.

The question then became this: "What do I do with that information?" My conclusion was clear, and undoubtedly wrong. The only way I could function in this world would be to put all that divine grandeur out of my mind. I couldn't allow myself to dwell on it. I'm being brutally honest. It was a massive failure on my part. It was a massive opportunity missed. Decades would go by before I was brought around by God to His glory, to the significance of the cross and resurrection, and to the existence and ministry of the Holy Spirit in a believer's life.

The Lord is "patient," but that word simply is inadequate. The Lord is "long-suffering," a much better word to describe my schooling, work, music, and all other activities in a carnal world. I use the term "carnal" not in the sense of perversion of the flesh, but simply the non-spiritual realm dependent on and limited by one's five senses. Put another way, having been exposed to the grandeur of the forest, I would spend decades digging around the bark of individual trees.

There were other "signals of transcendence" in 1968, the late-1990's, and big-time in late 2005. Let's work our way there.

14

Decision Time

I was happy in Huntingdon and at HAHS. High school had its challenges, but it wasn't too bad.

I had good friends in town, too, and I wasn't committing misdemeanors or felonies with them. They were nice, smart people, and I enjoyed being around them. Several of them I dated, not at the same time. At the obvious risk of omission, for which I apologize in advance, they were: Terry Stapleton, Arnie Saltzman, Bruce Kauffman, Kenny Hess, Steve Parks, Berwyn Reiter, Rich Reynolds, Nancy Snare, Pam Rhinesmith, "Cookie" Swigart, Dorrie Miller, Nancy Hall, Beth Shaffer, and Cathy Schmitt. Also, Diane DeMario from Mapleton. I had my learners permit and actually could drive the car around to explore nearby towns, like Pine Grove Mills, Mapleton, Ardenheim, and McConnellstown. Things were good.

My mother had other ideas. She was aware of the possible institution of a policy that a bad gym grade could knock you off Honor Roll. Moreover, Mother thought I was coasting a bit at HAHS. My argument was this: I wasn't first in the class. My friend Berwyn Reiter and some others always seemed to do better than I did. If I was competitive by nature and wasn't first in the class, how could I possibly be "coasting?" That logic seemed impeccable, but Mother did have a point.

As an English major in college, Mother also had some pedagogical problems with the way English was taught in certain quarters at HAHS. Teachers sometimes used expurgated versions of books, rather than the "real" versions. Mother thought that dumbed things down.

All this analysis on her part might have been academic (pun intended), but for the fact that there <u>was</u> an alternative to HAHS: a boarding school in Massachusetts called Mt. Hermon School.

The Day family in town were friends of our family. The father Hugh Day taught science at HAHS. One of the sons, Chris, a contemporary of my sister, had graduated from Mt. Hermon. He liked it a lot. It wasn't a snobby prep school. It had been founded by one of the evangelistic titans of the 19th Century, D. L. Moody, had mandatory chapel, a mandatory work program, and a dress code. It had a beautiful campus in the hills of central Massachusetts, and might be good for Sandy, Mother reasoned.

When she broached the matter to me in 1962, I was intrigued. We spoke with Chris Day about it, and he was enthused. I had to take the Secondary School Admission Test, and did OK, but my scores weren't stellar and may have revealed weaknesses in vocabulary, reading, and comprehension, validating some of Mother's concerns. We kept this all on the QT.

I applied, was accepted for the Fall of 1963, and received a scholarship. The name of the grant was the "William M. Tweed Scholarship." Was this an example of divine humor? Sandy with his history of bad behavior was the beneficiary of the largesse of the notorious "Boss Tweed." Mother surmised that D. L. Moody, founder of the school, must have tapped him for a contribution or two.

Mt. Hermon was a school for boys then; the sister school was Northfield School, a few miles away. The twain did not meet, except under supervision.

I decided to accept the offer from Mt. Hermon. Unbeknownst to me then, Mt. Hermon was to open doors for wonderful academic opportunities for me, indirectly leading me to my future wife Sheila seven years later.

Mt. Hermon Gateway Yearbook
1965.

15

"D.L. Moody's School"

There's no reason you should know this, but the title of this Chapter is intended as irony. The great evangelist D. L. Moody <u>did</u> establish Mt. Hermon and Northfield Schools (today combined under the name of Northfield Mt. Hermon School, or "NMH"), but neither school is really "D. L. Moody's School."

I am in a quasi-feud right now with the leadership at NMH. I argue that the school has become so secular and contrary to Christian principles that it shouldn't even mention D. L. Moody's name in the same breath or sentence as NMH. I've taken out ads in the nearby newspaper, and a few years ago wrote an article for the student newspaper on the subject. I argued that NMH should stop being just another prep school, and go back to its roots as a Christian school. It could be a beacon of Christian secondary education and provide a viable alternative to all the home-schooling going on in America now.

I insert that rant by way of contrast and comparison. Future Chapters of this book will explain how I got to this position. The "contrast" part involves the chasm between my thoughts now and what was in the mind of the McMeen kid leaving home to go to boarding school in 1963.

Mother drove me to Mt. Hermon, where I encountered the wonder of what looked like a college campus! No more going in and out of the same PA high-school building, with bells ringing for class changes. Mt. Hermon had expansive lawns, walkways, classroom buildings, a big gym, dormitories, a modern library, a chapel, and a dining hall. Down the hill in another direction was the school farm. It was impressive. I was excited.

An upperclassman greeted us, and showed us to my two-man room in the second floor of an aging, brick building called Crossley. I met my roommate, a very nice fellow from Paramus, NJ, named Blake Swan. I don't recall feeling intimidated. Mother left, and there I was.

In addition to the school, something else was new. I became "El" rather than Sandy. I wonder as I write this whether that reflected some major change in my being rather than just a name – whether it was somehow leaving all the youthful crimes and offenses behind, and really getting serious about life. The fact is that for the first time I was really on my own, living with a roommate, surrounded by guys and basically in the middle of nowhere. The mailing address for Mt. Hermon was Gill, Mass., which as far as I could tell didn't exist, or if it did, made McConnellstown, PA look like a metropolis.

The challenge for me in writing this is to give you a good picture of life at Mt. Hermon without making this a book on prep school. Did I like Mt. Hermon? There is no simple answer. A salient fact was that when my mother came to pick me up after Junior year there, the first words out of my mouth were, "Let's get out of here!" She had traveled hundreds of miles from Huntingdon and wanted a little tour. All I wanted to do was leave.

Mt. Hermon could be a really lonely place, even surrounded by all those fellow-travelers. The worst days were Sunday nights in the winter, with howling winds, snow, and nothing around, no family, no hometown friends, just a sense of desolation.

Maybe that is too dramatic; maybe I'm complaining. The reality was, however, that kids <u>did</u> run away from Mt. Hermon. Monday morning, we would discover that student X had disappeared; just left campus, never to return. Gone in the night. One legend was that a kid left on one of those wintry and snowy Sunday nights, and ended up in Cuba. That was pretty cool, actually.

Crazy things did happen at prep school, I must admit. A friend of mine there, a smart and funny guy named Mike Hannon, decided to go out the window onto the roof of the second floor of Crossley, and then was berated by a mutual friend Chris Martin for not jumping. ("Hannon, you chicken [expletive deleted], jump! You coward, jump!" On and on.) Mike, to his credit, didn't jump, but the whole thing was amusing to lonely prep school guys missing their families and hometown friends.

Academically, Mt. Hermon was dynamite. First-rate. Being a student there was an exercise in grade <u>deflation</u>. If you got in the high 80's at Mt. Hermon, you were a superstar. The high 90's that I had received at HAHS in English turned into 70's at first at Mt. Hermon. Mr. John P. Zilliax, a Harvard grad, taught 11th grade English, and my experience with expurgated books was exposed. We read works by Faulkner and Hemingway, and I had no clue. Especially Faulkner. I'd read "The Bear" and <u>The Sound and the Fury</u>, and I didn't know <u>what</u> was going on, what

73

was real and what was imaginary. I struggled, and that struggle continued into AP English Senior year with the wonderful terror of a teacher, T. D. Donovan.

Both 11th and 12th grade English at Mt. Hermon were rigorous, even college level, and there was no expurgation to make things easier.

If Mother wanted me to be "stretched," well, I was. I wasn't prepared for the so-called new SMSG math, so I took trigonometry Junior year. I scored in the high 90's, as I did in Latin II. The latter course was taught by an elderly gentleman Harold Stetson, who would write me a recommendation for college the next year. My grade average one term in Latin II was 99.6. Since I was a grade-grubber, I wanted it to be rounded up, but had to settle for a 99. Trigonometry and Latin II really helped my grade-point average.

While we are in the carnal realm, I want to confess that I wanted to make High Honor Roll at Mt. Hermon just once. Why? Because the "Hermonite" newspaper printed the names of all Honor Roll students, and the few who were High Honor Roll (with a 90 average) had their names printed in <u>Bold Print</u>. I really wanted that.

What put me over the top one marking period was an extra-credit project I did in Religion. That course was tough; Mr. Morgan was a hard grader. I can't remember the subject matter of my paper, but it earned me a 90 in the course that term, and I squeaked onto High Honor Roll, the only member of my class to make it that term as I recall. The entry from the Hermonite with my name in bold print is part of a collage Mother made for me on my Mt. Hermon experience.

I'm sure you are noting by now the vast distance between the grandeur of the Lord mentioned in Chapter 13 above, and my fixation on bold typeface.

Guys in our class like Paul Houston and Warren Ayres, who would be our Valedictorian and Salutatorian, respectively, were taking difficult math and science courses. I opted out of courses like physics and chemistry because I had them at HAHS (chemistry in summer school).

There were mini-disappointments at Mt. Hermon. My wife is tired of hearing me whine on one: The National Merit Scholarship Test. I got a 146 out of 160. In PA the cutoff for Semi-finalist was 145, but in Massachusetts, it was 147. I had to settle for a Letter of Commendation when someone with the same score in PA would be a Semi-finalist. OK, I never said I wasn't petty.

While we are wallowing in test scores and numbers, one of the happier days of my life was when I received my SAT achievement test scores between Junior and Senior years. I remember sitting on the steps of 1317 Moore Street and reading the numbers on the card. I did well enough in Spanish to opt out of college language courses, and got a 757 in Math II (which wasn't that hard) and a 738 in the English achievement (which was). Mt. Hermon informed me that I received the highest score in our class in the English achievement test. That info became highly relevant when a classmate later claimed that <u>he</u> had received a 756 in the English one. Hmmmm. He was outed, at least to me. I couldn't revel in the honor too long, since one fellow in our class got an 800 on that test as a Senior, consigning my mere 738 to the trash heap.

Some more funny stuff before we get serious. As my athletic endeavor, I was the "manager" of the excellent Mt. Hermon cross-country team. Basically, I got towels for the guys and kept a record of their finishing times. I was OK with the towels, but bad with the times. If five guys crossed the finish line within milli-seconds of each other, how in the heck could I record their precise times? Life wasn't digital then. The coach wasn't pleased with me.

On our team was a student by the name of Frank Shorter. After Yale, Frank went on to win the Marathon at the 1972 Olympics! I remember watching TV casually at the time, and a runner leading the pack was entering the stadium at Munich, and the announcer said it was Frank Shorter! What? Our Frank Shorter? From then on, my story was that I "managed Frank Shorter at Mt. Hermon."

The connection with the Northfield girls would warrant a book of its own. Included would be the supervised visits and protocol of allowing ten minutes of kissing, hugging, and other authorized (or excused) physical interaction in the parking lots after social events and before the buses would take the girls up the road and back to Northfield. We can leave it at that long sentence.

Music was a big part of the Mt. Hermon experience. The choral music was outstanding, and widely known among New England prep schools. Participation in the music programs had the added benefit that the boys and girls could make music together, so to speak.

The students put on two concerts a year: the Christmas Vespers concert and the Sacred Concert in the Spring. I have recordings of the Christmas Vespers concerts in 1964 and 1965, and they stand up after all these years. I can even remember some of the songs we sang. I was a second tenor in the larger chorus and in the A Cappella Choir. I played clarinet in the orchestra, too, and did some running back and forth during concerts so that I could do playing and singing.

The band situation was another matter. A teacher Mr. Carlton Stinchfield took on the responsibility of shaping up the band at Mt. Hermon. He and we band members tried valiantly. There were some good players, like our first-chair clarinet David Sibley, who had a great tone, but the overall strength wasn't there in the group. Coming from the great musical tradition in Huntingdon, with District Band and the shot at Regional, I was bummed out. My mother would send me the programs from District and Regional Bands in PA, and the names of my friends would show up, adding to my misery.

The band situation came to a head with what was to become in our class lore the notorious "West Side Story Concert." I can't remember exactly when it took place. Our band tackled a medley of tunes from "West Side Story." The music was over our head, with the dangerous combination of familiar and beloved melodies with syncopation and rhythms that were challenging Bernstein stuff. We crashed and burned. As we butchered song after song, pennies from the audience started raining down on the band. Our director was indignant, and strode off. Maybe we should have done "The Teddy Bears' Picnic" instead.

I caught a break on the instrumental side. David Sibley and I received quite an honor: we were selected to perform with a semi-professional orchestra in the area, The Pioneer Valley Symphony. We were permitted to go off campus and participate in the practices and concert with some really great players. The first clarinetist there had soloed with the Boston Symphony. Performing with that group was a real shot-in-the-arm for me, and a good addition to my college application.

Back to the choral singing. My experience with the A Capella Choir was a seminal event in my development as a guitarist. An A Cappella Choir doesn't have instrumental support; its power lies in its dynamics (loud and soft) and its rhythmic flexibility ("rubato"). The music has an ebb and flow, an arc, a sweep to it, and those characteristics seeped into my guitar playing in later years.

That brings us to guitar and my roommate Blake Swan. Blake provided my introduction to guitar. Thank you, Blake. There were some accomplished guitarists in our class, including Brian Ackerman (now Dr. Brian Ackerman). I actually had half a lesson with Brian. He wanted me to hold the guitar in a certain way (with my thumb behind the neck). His approach was quite proper, especially for playing in standard tuning with movable barre chords, but it just wasn't right for me.

Back to Blake. Blake loved playing guitar and singing. He also loved the song "Sloop John B," by the Kingston Trio. Our room was filled with guitar-playing and that particular song. Blake showed me some chords, and shared a lot of enthusiasm for the instrument. Those set me on my path as a guitarist.

Were there "signals of transcendence" for me at Mt. Hermon? Maybe not technically. What came pretty close, however, were the choral concerts, making wonderful music in a beautiful chapel, singing the song "Jerusalem" as a student body, and having the door opened by Blake to the world of guitar.

El's Mt. Hermon Yearbook Picture

16

Harvard? Really?

In early Fall 1964, Mr. Jervis W. Burdick, Jr. called me into his office. His nickname (behind his back, of course) was "Twig," and he was the Dean of Students at Mt. Hermon. He was very tall, usually with a cigarette, and bent slightly forward like Snoopy on his doghouse when he was imitating a bird-of-prey.

I hadn't committed any offenses it turned out; he just wanted to talk to me about college. "Where do you want to go?" he asked, smoke billowing forth. I mumbled something about large versus small, and then responded with "How about Harvard?" I really didn't know anything about Harvard except its reputation and that it was somewhere in or near Boston. I expected him to brush it off, and suggest something more realistic. Amazingly enough, he didn't. He was kind of offhand, and said, "Well, OK, that makes sense."

"You mean I really might have a shot at Harvard?!" That's what I was thinking. Me? Harvard?

Years later I contacted Mt. Hermon, and came right out and asked what my class rank was. The Archivist didn't hesitate to tell me. I was hoping for 4th, behind Houston, Ayres, and what I assumed was Mike Bressack. Their grades were stratospheric. I stood 6th in the class, taking account of weighting given to courses by difficulty. I consoled myself by remembering that I was there only two years, rather than three or four, and that I hadn't taken difficult science or math courses, except for Calculus.

At New England prep schools, we students had the luxury of interviewing on our campus with representatives of many colleges. We felt honored that colleges would send people to talk with us. I interviewed first with an older gentleman from Yale. (My father attended Yale, but never had enough credits to graduate.) The interviewer and I hit it off, and he gave me an A rating, out of A to C. That was a guaranty of admission unless I burned the school down and got caught.

Then I interviewed with Harvard, and things didn't go so well. The interviewer was a well-dressed, polished, preppy kind of guy, and I definitely wasn't. He gave me a B rating, out of A to E. Nine guys at Mt. Hermon got A ratings.

All this having taken place, I applied to just two colleges: Harvard and Yale. As I reflect on that ... *WAS I CRAZY??* Maybe not, but I was pretty trusting.

April 15th approached, and we students got word that the college letters would arrive on Monday. We also learned that nine students had been admitted to Harvard. I figured I was sunk. I went to a movie on campus over the weekend and tried to put the whole thing out of my mind.

Monday morning came, and two fat envelopes arrived: I got into Yale <u>and</u> Harvard! Harvard had apparently bounced a classmate with an A rating in favor of me, perhaps based on grades or recommendations. Yale gave me a scholarship.

It was a beautiful Spring day, and it was the happiest moment of my life. Other great life events -- marriage, children, jobs, grandchildren -- all involved massive doses of responsibility (well maybe not the grandchildren; they would just be fun, hopefully). This was the perfect day when a teenage kid got two fat envelopes from great universities when he expected only one. When I called my mother, I heard her screaming to my sister, "Sandy got into Harvard!"

Yale was a wonderful school, I got the scholarship, but my heart was set on Harvard. Mother said she'd find a way to pony up the $4k per year that Harvard cost back then.

An ancient Harvard sticker
I just found.

17

Harvard. Really.

As I try to tackle my life at Harvard and capture it in a Chapter or three, I face two matters right up front. First, I hope I'm not getting into the bad habit of writing books at night; I did that with the Steve Baughman book. I was up tonight at 1:42 AM, and I can't blame our cat Millie this time. She hadn't yet engaged in her usual practice of taking over the pillow around 2:30 every morning.

The tangible item I'm facing is a thin, maroon, hardbound book entitled "The Register," with the Harvard seal and "1969" on it. It is in rather good shape, showing some light scars, some water dots, and a large circular outline indicating that a hot or wet coffee cup had been placed on it in the last 50+ years.

The "1969" is misleading; the book was actually issued in 1965. It is the Freshman "facebook," a generic term back then for the publication containing pictures of what would be the Harvard Class of 1969. This book is a good summary or symbol of my experience at Harvard, or at least a place to start.

First, it's pretty classy. It could have been done in paperback but instead is bound with stitching that has lasted over half a century. Secondly, it contains an introduction by the Dean of Freshmen, notable in my eyes for having one of the greatest names I've ever encountered:

"F. Skiddy von Stade, Jr." I was too immature back then to be interested, but at my age now, writing this, I just <u>had</u> to find out: *What did the "F" stand for*? (It was "Francis.")

Besides the pictures of the Freshmen, The Register reflects some fascinating history by its exclusions and inclusions. As to exclusions: there are no female students pictured. Radcliffe College was part of Harvard then, but separate, and the Radcliffe gals had their own book. We guys, of course, rushed to get a hold of <u>their</u> book and pore over the pictures, fantasizing about possible date opportunities. Regarding inclusions, The Register pictured the graduate and law students who were "Freshman Proctors." Their responsibility back then seemed to be obtaining beer for the exceedingly underage Freshmen. (Maybe that's myth.) One of our Proctors went on to become a Justice of the Supreme Court of the United States, David Souter. He looks very serious in his picture.

The Register contains pictures of many young men who, from my perspective, would be frozen in time. I wouldn't know them at Harvard, but they would go on to graduate, live productive lives with family and vocations of various types, and in more and more cases pass away and be memorialized in the obit section of the Harvard Magazine. To me many of those whom I didn't know personally will always be the teenagers pictured in The Register. When I would read their obituaries, my mind would go back to their youthful, hopeful, and earnest-looking faces in The Register.

But Harvard was a blast, too, and The Register gives a hint of the fun and joy I would have as a Harvard student. The first Freshman entry in The Register was suspicious: a student named "Ahman Abelone," whose major was stated as "Oceanography." On the next page appeared "Phols Alarm," whose major was to be "Pyrotechnics." Somebody at Harvard had a sense of humor!

The book also contained ads for coin-operated laundry services, typewriter rentals (!), and the Star Pharmacy boasting of free deliveries and reasonable prices for the Harvard student whose organic chemistry course (the notorious Chem 20) would give him palpitations and a serious headache.

Finally, The Register gave phone listings for women's colleges in the area. Those proved useful.

The most famous person in our class, for at least the six months he was there, was the rock star Gram Parsons, who went on to fame and some fortune with Emmylou Harris, The Byrds, and the Flying Burrito Brothers. I, of course, having been in the cocoon of Mt. Hermon School, had never heard of him. He died, sadly, at age 26 of an overdose in a motel in Joshua Tree, California.

Tommy Lee Jones was yet to become a film star, and Al Gore was just the son of a US Senator. I heard, by scuttlebutt, of a phenomenal clarinetist in our class, who had soloed with the Boston Symphony. (He was not the clarinetist who played with the Pioneer Valley Symphony, if you were wondering. If you actually <u>were</u> wondering, I'm really impressed!) He had the distinguished name of John Adams, and went on to become a Pulitzer Prize-winning composer.

One of my classmates had a moniker even more relevant to our college; his name was John Harvard. Really. His name was not made up for The Register. He was John Tyler Harvard. I can't imagine what would have happened to John if he had gone to Yale.

Harvard itself was like an oasis plopped down in the middle of a good-size city. Harvard Square was full of businesses and buildings right off the sidewalk, and people who walked fast and were, or pretended to be, Harvard students. As soon as you passed through one of the gates to the Harvard Yard, however, the atmosphere abruptly changed. It was quiet and even bucolic, assuming that the "Spring Riots" or other student demonstrations weren't taking place.

Freshmen lived in the Yard first year, and then ended up at the several dormitories, called "Houses." My Freshman dorm was Wigglesworth, and my House was to be Leverett House Towers, a few blocks from the Yard and near the Charles River.

After settling into Room A-12 of Wigglesworth, which backed onto a sidewalk along Massachusetts Avenue, I met two classmates. First was Carl Vigeland, a good-looking guy from Buffalo, trumpet-player, with great hair. In later life he would write two of the most informative and entertaining books about musicians I would ever read: In Concert: Onstage and Offstage with the Boston Symphony Orchestra (Morrow, 1989), covering Charles Schlueter, Principal Trumpet of the BSO, and Jazz in the Bittersweet Blues of Life (DaCapo Press, 2001), covering Wynton Marsalis.

The second classmate was Marty Chalfie. Not only was he an ace student at a large suburban Chicago high school, he was a state swimming star and an accomplished classical guitarist. Wow. We had fun tackling Geoff Muldaur's guitar tune called "Mole's Moan" together. Marty and I have stayed in touch over the years on musical matters. He has recorded at my house, and I had the music mastered. It was that good. Oh, and he also accomplished a little something called the "Nobel Prize in Chemistry" in 2008, while he was a tenured professor at Columbia.

One time later that first day I overheard an animated conversation between classmate Irwin Gaines and classmate Simeon Taylor. They were speaking in the English language, but I didn't understand any of the words. It had to do with some esoteric mathematical matter. I had good reason to be scared: Irwin had reputedly won (that is WON) the National Mathematics Competition, and Simeon would go on to become Valedictorian of our class.

Just to show my massive ignorance, when Simeon introduced himself to me, I thought his name was spelled "Simian." Boy, was I wrong, and worse yet, completely ignorant of the various Simeons in the Bible. There's a line in the Woody Allen movie "Love and Death" where the young Woody's character shakes his head and says about his father, "He was an idiot, but I loved him!" Think God as Woody (well, just for this very limited point), and me as the father.

My roommates appeared. John Duffy came from Boston, got there as the early bird, and claimed the worm – namely, the bedroom with the single bed. Duff was and is a great human being, very compassionate. He was always trying to set me up on dates. He eventually became a priest, and the President of "The Missionary Society of St. Paul the Apostle" (the Paulist Fathers) in the US. Being from central PA where we talk deliberately (OK, slowly), I had a hard time keeping up with fast Boston-ese that issued from the mouth of Duff. He later picked up Spanish, and even preached and ministered in Spanish. I bet he could talk muy rápido in Español!

Arriving later was one George Alphonso Booth, III. In my paperwork, I had requested a roommate who played clarinet and was from a public school in the Midwest. George fit the bill. He was from Beaumont High, St. Louis, MO, and was African-American. George's nickname became "Bullet," since his head resembled a bullet. I'm not sure who came up with that; maybe George but probably Duffy.

George and I rubbed each other the wrong way from the get-go. We were both highly insecure, and exacerbating the situation for me was that he could talk and think faster than I could. When we had arguments on just about every subject, he was disturbingly logical, and his conclusions always seemed to conflict with mine. He was also very adept at employing "ethnic" jargon to pounce on me:

El: "Bullet, you're an idiot!"
George: "Your momma's an idiot!"

I'd jump in to defend "my momma," and the situation would deteriorate. My schooling at Mt. Hermon hadn't afforded me an adequate response to the "your momma" argument.

There was a funny, yet sad, epilogue to all this. George and I changed roommates; I stayed with Duff, and got a third roommate, Doug Yock, who transferred in from St. Olaf College. More about that super-star later. I met George at our 25th reunion in 1994, and we really bonded, and got a huge kick out of each other. After that reunion, George would fly into NYC from the West Coast, and we would have dinner and go to shows together in the City. We became really fond of each other, and had a great time revisiting and laughing over all the agita in our Freshman year. Sadly, George had a heart attack and died in February 1997, robbing us of future good times together.

The person who called me in 1997 to report on George's death was my third roommate, Douglas Harold Yock, Jr. Doug looked like a male model, had been a Presidential Scholar, one of two from Minnesota, and was another star swimmer like Marty Chalfie. He was a Chemistry major, and his academic performance at Harvard was spectacular. After receiving a grade of 20 (out of 100) on his first exam in the aforementioned Chem 20 (which was a typical grade for the first test in that course), he went on to receive grades like 95 and 98. We would get these little post cards with our exam and final grades on them, and Doug would get A's, 98's, 97's, numbers like that. I told him that Duff and I could handle the stratospheric grades; it was the sycophantic comments from the graders that galled us. "Doug, I want you to do research with me!" "Doug, please come to Harvard Grad School!" "Doug, please have my baby!" (OK, I just threw in that last one.) We were kidding, of course. We bragged Doug up all over Campus. He went on to graduate second in our class, just behind Simeon, and get his M.D. from Harvard Med School.

As for academics, in a non-grade-inflation (I claim) environment, I tended to end up with a B+. The one C+ I got was in, of all things, pre-law.

I had a simple problem. I never seemed to do well in the mid-term "hour exams." I couldn't get my act together in an hour. I don't know why. I would do a lot better in the three-hour finals, but the A- in the final wouldn't sufficiently raise the mid-term B- to the rarefied A- level. Still a B+ average put you in Group II out of six, and that was easily on Dean's List, which I managed to make every term at Harvard. Dean's List provided fodder for headlines and articles in the Huntingdon Daily News, lovingly typed by you-know-whom: my mother.

I graduated with an Honors called "cum laude in general studies." That basically meant in the non-scientific majors that you had good grades, but didn't have the motivation (read: you were too lazy) to write a Senior Thesis to get a Magna or Summa. Officially, I was in the top 20% of the class, but my own grade-grubbing and highly unofficial interpolation placed me higher. In any event, I missed Phi Beta Kappa, which was top 10%. In later years, my wife would love to hold up and read in my presence the Phi Beta Kappa newsletter (called the "Key Reporter") that arrived at our door in <u>her</u> name. Grrr.

As to courses at Harvard, I started out as a Math major. I mistook my early A in Calculus for intelligence when it was really more about having learned the subject matter at Mt. Hermon. After that, my grades were, in math terms, monotonically decreasing, down to a B in the Analysis course, first term Sophomore Year.

I was absolutely clueless in that Analysis course. It was taught by a genius named Andrew Gleason. During a lecture one time, he stopped to ponder something. He had said "n-dimensional space" when he really meant "infinite-dimensional space." My blood ran cold; this guy not only could <u>visualize</u> those concepts, he could <u>distinguish</u> them! The afternoon of the final in that course, I went to the administration building and, presto-changeo, turned into a History major. I also went out and bought a 12-string guitar; more about that later.

There is an epilogue to the story of the disturbing Analysis course. Years later at a Harvard-Yale football game in New Haven, I ran into a really bright classmate and friend of mine, who had been in the Harvard Analysis class, later graduated from Yale Law, and was working as a lawyer in DC. I was lamenting my experience in the Analysis course. He interrupted to say that *no one in the course knew what was going on*! It seems that Professor Gleason thought that Professor Birkhoff in the earlier part of the program had covered certain material, when he hadn't. When I told my friend that I received a B in the Analysis course, he was impressed. It seems that most people had done worse. Now, tell me that wasn't a God-at-work moment! For 20 years I had considered myself, unjustly, as a Math dolt.

At Harvard I didn't exactly go around seeking out the most demanding courses, or, God forbid, "auditing" anything. Auditing meant you attended classes for the fun of it. I left that to the go-getters at Radcliffe.

One year I got interested in fine arts. A favorite course for those students growing weary of intellectual challenge

93

was "Fine Arts 171: 20th Century Painting," known affectionately as "Darkness at Noon." Students would pile into the auditorium and watch movies and pictures of paintings on the screen. The Professor would educate us on things like "chiaroscuro" and "figures," which he pronounced "figgers" for some reason. Those figgers were often unclad women, but since this was 20th century art, their body parts, if any, had odd shapes and appeared in the wrong places.

I wrote a paper on Paul Klee and received an A-. I was hoping for an A, which would have rhymed with Klee. That was during Spring term of my Sophomore year.

Spring term of my Senior year I was accepted at law school and was drifting into academic ennui. I signed up for a course on 19th Century Intellectual History, taught by Professor Crane Brinton. At the first lecture, 200 or so students (including most members of the football team) crowded into the auditorium. Crane (as he was affectionately called) informed us that we could either attend his lectures or read his book. There would be no final exam, just a paper required for the course. I counted 20 (that's not a typo) attendees at his next lecture, which would be the last one for me. I read the book but don't remember anything about it except that there was a picture of an egg on the front.

In thinking about the assignment, my mind turned to the A- I had received on the Paul Klee paper in Fine Arts 171.Hmmmm. Perhaps the learning in that exercise might "inform" my work on the paper for Crane's course. Let's not dig too deeply into what the previous sentence meant in actual practice. I did create a new couple of introductory paragraphs, and then "imported the wisdom" of the rest of the Klee paper into the paper for Crane's course.

When I got the paper back, the grad student who had graded it wrote the following: "B-. I don't see how this relates to the subject matter of the course." His mind had apparently gone "tilt" at how exactly a paper on 20th century art fit into a course on 19th century intellectual history.

Before you get indignant and judgmental, I <u>did</u> have some ammo for my position. The assignment for the paper didn't "technically" require the paper to be on the subject matter of the course. I was on my way to law school, pounced on that, quoted the assignment, and appealed the B- to Professor Brinton himself. I can hardly believe now that I had the chutzpah to do that. He responded on a little piece of paper I remember to this day: "I agree. A-." I think Crane just loved the students; it was that simple, and rare.

Franklin "El-model" guitar (2017).

18

Music at Harvard

When the discussion turns to music at Harvard, I am both clear <u>and</u> fuzzy on the subject. The clarity regards my clarinet-playing; the fuzzy part involves the guitar.

The Harvard Band was quite an institution at Harvard. The band would perform often hilarious half-time shows at the Ivy League games. It would mock the other school and team in high-handed and hateful terms ("Har-vard Re-jects, Har-vard Re-jects"). It would, in addition, engage in a certain ribald brand of humor that delighted the undergrads and dismayed the administration and the Old Grads. For example, the band might form on the field something vaguely resembling a part of the human anatomy, while playing music oozing double-entendre.

The band also mocked the established, traditional college marching bands with their studied precision and marching skill. Instead of marching in righteous progression and lines, when the Harvard Band needed to change positions, someone would shoot off a cap gun, and the kids would run to the next position in mirthful chaos. I loved the band, as did many or most Harvard students at the games.

My problem was that I couldn't really march, and even with the band's loose definition of order, I couldn't hack it. I tried out for and made the "Concert Band." What a blessing!

I got a maroon "Harvard Band" sport jacket that I could wear all over the world to show off that I went to Harvard. I'm not sure the fit was perfect, but the Harvard "H" on it was big.

The Concert Band was comprised of good, smart players, had a good sound, and played together well. There were no "West Side Story" debacles, a la Mt. Hermon.

We had some interesting gigs. We did concerts in Cleveland, Ohio, and Troy, New York. The venues weren't exactly Carnegie Hall, but the concerts were attended by hordes of appreciative and vociferous alumni/ae.

The most memorable gig was the famous/notorious "Lowell Golden Gloves Tournament." People who live in Lowell, Mass. know it well. The band would play between bouts. Interestingly enough, each bout seemed to pit a black boxer against a white boxer. I couldn't figure that out, but that's my recollection.

The boxers would fight, starting with the little guys. Then we would play. Then bigger guys would rumble; then we would play. Problems started to develop after a while. The fans seemed to get more and more inebriated as the boxing ascended in weight class. By the middleweights, the fans discovered that it was fun to throw empty beer cans at the band. We were in some kind of cage, which didn't afford full protection. By the light heavyweights, disgruntled customers were throwing cans at the band that were not empty. Our Conductor Jim Walker thought it might be a good time to exit.

Now to guitar. The fuzzy part is that I believe that I had become somewhat accomplished on guitar, but I can't remember where, when, or how I did it. Marty Chalfie and I were playing "Mole's Moan," as mentioned earlier, but I can't remember when I learned it. Was it the summer after Mt. Hermon, when my mother got me my first decent guitar – an all-mahogany Gibson, for $50? I remember fingerpicking with clanky, metal fingerpicks, but don't know how or when or from whom I learned.

I do remember receiving some valuable instruction from David Shaffer, a really bright Huntingdon fellow who was Valedictorian of the HAHS Class of 1964, a really strong wrestler, and, as if that weren't enough, played guitar well. (I saw David doing one-arm pullups on a high-bar once, and never forgot it.) He taught me how to play with one finger (the middle one; don't go there) and a thumb, rather than three fingers and a thumb. That really helped me, and I played that way for twenty years until I found it limiting in the 1980's.

At the beginning of Sophomore year, I abruptly gave up clarinet in favor of guitar. After playing that instrument since 4th grade, I never picked it up again. I went cold-turkey. It was guitar or nothing.

One time when I was lamenting to my mother that I didn't take advantage of all the cultural opportunities at Harvard, she cut to the chase: "That's because you were learning to play guitar." She was right. Without music, any teaching tapes, any books, I was messing around with guitar, and singing folk songs. I would sing and play in the stairwell at Leverett House, where the acoustics were big if not very refined. I'd practice music for hours. A classmate

Dave Ament amazed me with his version of "A'Soaling" by Peter, Paul, and Mary, and I tried to learn that. I did Phil Ochs songs; I did Gordon Lightfoot songs; I did Tom Rush, a musical hero who had graduated from Harvard a few years earlier. I even tried to sing like Bob Dylan sometimes. I spent hours of undisciplined time with guitar every day at Harvard. I even gave lessons to some talented youngsters, including John Nordell, son of dear friends of ours, whom we met in Cambridge.

As a Senior, I got up the courage to play out a bit. I remember a gig when I played and sang at a kid's birthday party. The din was unbelievable and nobody was paying the least attention to my efforts on stage. The mother seemed satisfied, so I got my $25. I would play and sing under a tree in the Harvard Yard, and attract a small, appreciative crowd.

Regarding guitars, I went from the mahogany Gibson to a beautiful sunburst Gibson Hummingbird, which I bought at a store in Harvard Square. It cost $135, and after a down-payment, I paid $5 a week. It seemed forever before it was paid for, during which time it sat in the window of the store.

As mentioned earlier, I bought a wonderful Guild 12-string as a reward to myself for leaving Math and becoming a History major. I traded a guitar for a Martin 000-28, and finally got a Martin D-21 in 1968. I may have forgotten a guitar or two. My friend John Kennedy (John <u>E</u>. Kennedy) drove me to a store in the North End where I bought the D-21 for $180, give or take. That guitar was to last me for 17 years.

I was always short of money at Harvard, even though I worked a fair number of hours at Widener Library. Guitars were the money pit, so I treat that matter here.

I was able to work my way out of money problems in two ways. First involved "wide-wale corduroy pants." My mother put me in touch with a merchant in Huntingdon, Ted English, who owned a clothing store and was a pretty snappy dresser himself. Ted had gotten in a quantity of wide-wale corduroy trousers, but they were a bust in Huntingdon. At Harvard, however, they were the bomb. I bought all of Ted's wide wales at $3 per, and sold them at Harvard for $15 per. They just flew out of my dorm room. The students didn't even care if they fit; they had to have those corduroys!

The second method for debt extinguishment involved my two student tickets to what was to be the greatest Harvard-Yale football game in history. Each team was undefeated, and they met for the Ivy league championship in November 1968. Investment bankers in Boston were offering exorbitant prices for these tickets. I succumbed and sold my two at the Harvard Club of Boston for $150 cash — tremendous bucks back then. After the sale, however, I concluded that I wanted to go to the game, so I bought a ticket from an SDS member (the radical student organization back then) for $5. The game ended in a tie, 29-29, after Harvard's great comeback by 16 points in a matter of minutes at the end of the game. That was the first and only time I would run onto a football field with a mass of humanity after a game. Kevin Rafferty made a great film on the game, called "Harvard Beats Yale, 29-29," quoting the famous headline in the Harvard Crimson student newspaper after the game.

An epilogue to this story: at our 5th class reunion, in 1974, a classmate with a few drinks in him approached me and berated me for selling my Harvard-Yale tickets in 1968. I was surprised that he remembered or cared. I told him I had bought a ticket from another student and was at the game. He shuffled off, his sodden indignation nevertheless intact I suspect.

19

God and Church at Harvard

Harvard, founded in 1636 to educate and produce Christian ministers, has tried to finesse that fact. For example, the little spiral-bound handbook (the "Harvard Handbook") given to us innocent Freshmen in 1965 contains this grandiose statement on page 17:

"Harvard University was founded in 1636 to continue the tradition of English civilization and culture in the newly settled colonies of New England."

If I had been at all mature in my Christian faith at that time, which I wasn't, I would have declared balderdash or worse on that statement. Harvard had lost its spiritual soul to secularism and academic prowess.

Things were not so bad as my more conservative friends might think. The professors weren't there with the singular purpose of filling young, impressionable minds with Satan-worship or other demonic ideas. There were some presuppositions, of course, like the importance of a strong U.S. President (unless, of course, the faculty didn't _like_ the particular President at the time), and a fair amount of liberal thought. Mostly, faculty and students were absorbed in doing their respective "things:" the faculty teaching, but really yearning for more time and grants to do research in their respective fields, and the students worried about keeping up with their coursework. (In History, for example, I had to read hundreds, even thousands, of pages a week.)

Religion was available on campus for all types of believers or unbelievers. I attended the nearby University Lutheran Church a couple of times, and was on their mailing list for 40 years thereafter until they finally gave up on me. The Harvard chapel was very simple and beautiful and I spent a few Sunday mornings there.

That having been said, a pattern was developing in my life. There was "religion" -- meaning, church, Sunday school, organized things like that -- and there were "spiritual matters," including the "signals of transcendence" discussed in Chapter 13. Religion and spiritual matters (or, in the latter case, a relationship with God through the ministry of the Holy Spirit) would not intersect in my life until I was in my 50's. That was not to happen at Harvard, but some things of significance <u>did</u> happen. I experienced my second "signal of transcendence" there.

It all started with a visit my Senior year by a family friend Betsy Taylor. I showed her around Harvard and a bit of Boston. It wasn't a date, just a nice get-together with a good gal from a good family. Her maternal Grandmother was the beloved "Mother Daniels" in Huntingdon.

We were on our way to an Italian restaurant in the North End of Boston when we encountered a fellow begging on the street. I entered protective mode, and positioned myself to walk around him, shielding Betsy. She had different ideas, and showed the amazing compassion of Jesus to that man, which had a profound impact on me. I was to e-mail her later and declare that her attitude there and then led me to a born-again experience. It really didn't, I now believe. (The e-mail bounced anyway, as I recall, or at least Betsy didn't respond to it.) It was instead -- you guessed it -- a "signal of transcendence."

I know that because after Betsy left, I had a very strange experience when I returned to my dorm. I went into the dining room at Leverett House, and it was as if I were looking through a prism at what was otherwise an ordinary day of students getting their food, sitting down, talking, and laughing. There was a separation going on. It was if I were looking at something from a different world. It wasn't simply that I had returned to the ordinary Harvard life after a charming lady had shown compassion to a homeless person. There was no spirit of condemnation or judgmentalism in my heart regarding my fellow students. There was a spirit of separation, of being of a different world from what I was seeing. It was indeed a "signal of transcendence." It wasn't in a church, nor was it an emotional reaction to singing, playing, or listening to Christian music.

On the other hand, it was not fully realized. It was a seed of something that started to sprout in the mid-1990's, and then bloom in November 2005. I was age 21 then; in November 2005 I was 58.

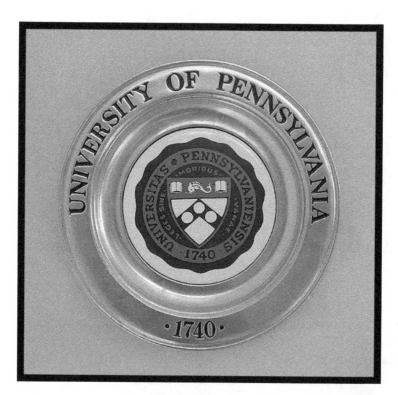

Penn plate.

20

Law School

Right now, I feel a bit like my Huntingdon High School teacher Harvey McElhoes. He was the one who expressed enthusiasm for the "World Cultures" course he taught while admitting he was staying three pages ahead of the students. As I write this memoir, I am discovering connections and themes as the story unfolds. That is the case concerning the eminent "University of Pennsylvania Law School," in Philadelphia, PA.

I cannot jump to Philly right away; I need to discuss the process of my ending up at Penn. That is a key ingredient of some God-at-work manna that I argue the Lord dropped on one Sheila Taenzler and me. I contend that the Lord moved the pawns in the chess game, and we were the pawns. Sheila is really a queen, of course, but for present purposes both of us were the acted-upon rather than the actors.

Back to Harvard. I didn't want to go to Grad School and spend five years getting a Ph.D. I simply wasn't that interested in any particular academic subject. I didn't want to go right to work because I didn't know what kind of work to do. Despite my success in the sale of two football tickets and numerous corduroy pants, I didn't consider myself much of a businessman.

Issues concerning the draft and the Vietnam War were raging, about which everyone was inflamed one way or another. I received a 4-F exemption due to my CP. The doctor who wrote me the letter said he was in favor of the war, but he wouldn't want me fighting alongside his son if he were called. I fully got his drift.

Law school was the logical choice. I had a further reason, which sounded abstract at the time but turned out to be right on the money. Law seemed to provide a combination of the rigor of math with a degree of social significance in a world of real people and their challenges and problems. Your brain would be fully occupied, and you could still have an effect on society. That was an oddly prescient analysis for me at my level of maturity then. I believe it came from the Lord. It wasn't a "signal of transcendence," but instead some actual wisdom the Lord bestowed on me. It proved out in three years of law school, and 28 years of law practice in New York City.

I took the Law School Admission Test, and for the first time since the Secondary School Admission Test for Mt. Hermon, I didn't do that well in a standardized test. I did a terrible job of proceeding through the exam at a steady, timely pace, finished only about 2/3ds of the questions, and received a score at the 75th percentile. That wasn't terrible, but knocked me out of the running at Harvard or Yale, where just about every aspiring law student in my class wanted to go. I made Wait List at Harvard, but that was it.

I applied additionally to Michigan Law, Chicago Law, Cornell Law, and Penn Law. I was accepted relatively quickly by Michigan, Chicago, and Cornell. Time passed, and I kind of forgot about Penn.

One day it hit me that I hadn't heard from Penn. I picked up the phone and called the Admissions Office to see whether they had made a decision on my application. After a short discussion, a man got on the phone. It was Arnold Miller, the Dean of Admissions at Penn! I was honored he would even talk to me, a mere college supplicant. He was very nice, asked for my grades, and asked for my boards. There was a pause, while he seemed to do some back-of-the-envelope analysis. He then got back on the phone and said, "You're in!"

I was really thrilled with that level of personal attention and, frankly, his interest in me. After the law board fiasco, I was a wounded soul. Arnie gave me just what I needed, a real boost. I accepted the offer.

Penn Law Yearbook – Class of 1972.

21

Penn Law School

Many members of my generation were attending a rock and roll festival at Yasgur's Farm, near Woodstock, NY, in the summer of 1969. I was doing something more mundane in that sweltering summer. I was living in a room of an un-air-conditioned house in Cambridge, Mass. and working at the Harvard School of Education library. It was a little respite in Cambridge before the next chapter of my life, at law school.

Philly was like a small town in the guise of a large city. With its grid pattern and logic in layout, it was a lot easier to drive in than Boston. Since I had no car in college, I didn't have to drive around much in Beantown, with its involuted, narrow streets and many incompetent and impatient drivers, some of whom were undoubtedly educated at Harvard. (In NYC, drivers would be equally impatient, but generally more competent if more aggressive.)

Philly was rougher than Cambridge. It perhaps wasn't "stormy, husky, brawling," words applied by Carl Sandburg to Chicago in the poem of that name, but it was muscular. It may have been the presence of the train tracks in West Philly, the urban blight, or rough roadways (before the city made infrastructure improvements in connection with the celebration of the Bicentennial in 1976).

I shared an apartment with a pot-smoking Penn Freshman (I did not indulge), on West 43d Street, directly across from the Fairfax Apartments where an elderly aunt of my mother's had lived years before. That was an interesting coincidence. I don't know whether it was of God, because the place was burglarized, I had some valuable items stolen, and I ended up moving to 222 West Rittenhouse Square in Center City.

An impoverished law student living on Rittenhouse Square, you say? Well, yes, but only with a roommate, and only in a building that might be called "down at the heels" but that would mean that it <u>had</u> heels. It technically did have a doorman, if that's what one would call the huge, squat, glowering individual sitting at the front desk with his black, menacing dog.

Law school was a sort of regression, closer somewhat to elementary school than to college. We had a book for each course, and we sat in assigned seats, so that the professors could call on and humiliate individuals by name, Mr. or Miss so-and-so. That approach was to keep people like me from cowering in the back, furtive and trying to remain anonymous.

The Penn Law building on 34th Street had a new part and an old part. The old part was classy, with stone and ornaments -- sort of Greece-and-Rome-Go-Philly style. The new part was well-lighted if a little bland. The Men's Room on the first floor in the new part had the funniest and most erudite graffiti I've ever read on a john wall – much better than the crude stuff in Widener Library at Harvard. If I hadn't been busy there, I would have written some of it down to share with you here. It was that good.

First year law school was an exercise in forcing the students to be really clear and precise in their thinking. College, at least in the Humanities, was a piece of cake next to law school. In college you read thousands of pages, and before the final re-read as much as possible, and then spilled out on the bluebook what you could remember. In law school it was more intensive than extensive; more laser beam than floodlamp. I simplify, but that's close.

In law school, you would have to analyze how a court came to a decision on a set of facts, and then vary the facts and see whether that would change the decision. To do that, you really had to home in on the reasoning of the court. That could be difficult because often courts would engage in "dicta," meaning statements that were really not germane to the decision in the case. The law professors pounded into us to concentrate on what the court <u>did</u> in a case — namely, who won and who lost — and not to get unduly caught up in the eloquence or literary quality of the judge writing the opinion.

All that being said, students on their own would discover judges who wrote well. There were titans like Justice Louis Brandeis of the Supreme Court of the United States, and Judge Henry Friendly of the Second Circuit Court of Appeals, which sat in New York. Then there was our own Justice Michael Musmanno, a colorful character who wrote some entertaining opinions while sitting on the Supreme Court of Pennsylvania.

Some of the large books in the library would fall open to judicial opinions beloved by students, whether for the quality of the writing or for the facts of the case, especially if those facts involved sex or some unusual type of mayhem.

At Penn Law I discovered that an ancient relative of mine, one William Josiah McMeen, was the basis for a Pennsylvania Supreme Court decision on a very important legal issue. The court held that a defendant could indeed be convicted of murder based on circumstantial evidence. Josiah was a bad guy who poisoned his wife. He was hanged. But he did give rise to that groundbreaking legal principle in PA. I, of course, bragged up that bad boy to my classmates.

Back to the pedagogy of first-year law school. Let's say a court held for the Plaintiff ·· the suing party ·· in a case with facts A, B, C, and D. Well, what would the same court do if the facts instead were B, C, D, and E? For the typical law student, at the end of first year you were almost completely bewildered and ready to canonize your professors since they seemed like the smartest people in the world as they deftly changed facts on us, asked us unanswerable questions, and looked smug, with arms crossed.

My Criminal Law course first year was taught by a Penn legend Louis (pronounced "Louie") B. Schwartz. We were scared and serious students, so no one to my knowledge saw the connection between Louis B. Schwartz and the Chuck Berry song "Johnny B. Goode."

Louis wore pink shirts and bow ties and was both smooth and jocular. In his class first term, we studied one case for two whole weeks – Fain v. State. The facts of that case in my imperfect recollection boil down to these: Someone woke up a sleeping individual at a train station, and Mr. Sleeper responded by shooting Mr. Waker dead.

Was Mr. Sleeper/Fain guilty of murder? That was the question.

Mushy, collegiate brains had to be led by the cerebrum through matters of intention, motivation, causation, liability, etc., etc. and what turned out to be the deciding fact: volition. Mr. Fain didn't act volitionally; therefore, he wasn't guilty of murder. It's as if you walked in your sleep and kicked someone in a wheelchair into traffic. Mr. Fain also must have had a <u>very</u> good lawyer.

After I came to know the Lord in 2005, that concept of volition really helped me on some theological matters with which I was wrestling. Who would have guessed that Mr. Fain and his pistol had anything to do with Calvinism or Arminianism, but they did for me.

The students at Penn Law were smart, but more buttoned-down and less wild-and-wooly than the students who had been charging around Harvard Yard when I was there scant months earlier.

There were practice exams first term. I did poorly on them, of course, per my history at Harvard. The exams at the end of the first year were for all the marbles: one exam in each course, and that was your grade. All five credits in each major course -- Property, Criminal Law, Civil Procedure, Torts, and Contracts -- would ride on one long exam. Even with number grades having been earlier discontinued at Penn, there still were "real" grades: D for Distinguished (none, or max one a course); E for Excellent, maybe top 20%; G for Good, next 30%; Q for Qualified, next 50%; and U for Unqualified, if you really blew the exam.

Right before final exams in 1970, the shootings at Kent State University took place. In a tense situation, members of the Ohio National Guard shot into crowds of unarmed students, killed four, and wounded nine. Students throughout the country were in an uproar. Penn Law offered the option of taking exams Pass-Fail for students too upset to perform on the exams. A fair number took their exams Pass-Fail. I was tempted, but ending up taking them for grades. That was the right decision for me, as things turned out.

The closest I got to spiritual matters or religion during that school year was that I was befriended by three lovely ladies. They were ex-nuns, studying at the nursing school, who fed me periodically and well, and provided solace. I met the one lady on the street next to the Law School, and as fate would have it, her name was in the Philadelphia phone book right next to mine: Christine McMenamin. Nice folks, all of them. Otherwise, I have to confess that I had more of an overt relationship with Fain in that period than with my heavenly Father.

I made good friends at the law school first year: some from Harvard like Jack Fitzgerald and Chris Gallagher; from Lehigh, Paul Levy and Tom Hunt; from Penn State, Jay Gurmankin; from Illinois, Keith Armour; from Penn, Lou Corsi; and from Holy Cross, Cornelius ("Connie") Finnegan. We basically studied day and night for the whole school year. It was relentless.

I know there's been a lot of talk about grades in this book. That will soon end, because I will wrap up discussion of formal schooling shortly.

I took my exams, and did well. Penn wouldn't tell me how well. I received American Jurisprudence awards for best grade in my section (there were two sections) in Property and Civil Procedure. I made Law Review, an important honorary organization in law school that is a very helpful credential for getting a good law job. Basically, I peaked academically first year in law school. That was really helpful for an aspiring lawyer. Praise God. I still had problems finishing exams, but first year exams were mainly tests of your ability to spot legal issues in fact situations. I had gone wild on the exams, issue-spotting like a madman, and the professors apparently cut me slack. Praise God again.

My grades in law school were to decline subsequently, which was fairly typical for members of Law Review (except for Sheila, of course, whose went up). We spent countless hours on the review cite-checking articles, writing short legal pieces called Comments or longer pieces called Notes, and generally helping get the issues out. I managed to graduate with Honors from Penn Law. I had to take my third year at Columbia Law School in New York City because a certain lady had become front and center in my life.

University of Pennsylvania
Law Review

FOUNDED 1852

Formerly
American Law Register

22

Sheila Ann Taenzler

I earlier wrote that the happiest day of my life was the day I got into Harvard. I need to modify that statement. That was the "co-happiest" day with today, when I get to write a Chapter in my memoirs about Sheila Ann Taenzler, who would become my wife in 1971.

In the Fall of 1970, I set foot in the hallowed offices of the "University of Pennsylvania Law Review," along with the other newbies who had just made Review. Some of our class members were astounded at who made it. Many of us were the quiet, almost invisible types who tried to keep a low profile in class. We didn't argue with the professors, and didn't hang around the cafeteria or the iconic metal "Goat" statue in the law school commons. One malcontent, sucking on a cigarette, scoffed at the people who made Review, declaring that we were "incompetent." Even a Martian could taste sour grapes in that one.

One of my first acts in the Review offices was to check the list of new members and verify the spelling of my name. In the Harvard Yearbook for the Class of 1969, the printer had managed to mix up the names and pictures of some of my classmates. I was one of them, to my mother's great annoyance. (She had paid full retail for my Harvard education and we deserved a better yearbook, she claimed, quite reasonably.) You will see the picture of Sean McCarthy next to my name in the Harvard Yearbook, and my picture next to Mike Marean's name. In any event, I wanted to make sure my name was spelled right as an "Associate Editor" for the Masthead of the Law Review.

I wasn't the only person looking at the names. Another was a lady in the class ahead of me. She was one of the few women who had made Law Review the previous year. (In subsequent years, more women would attend law school, and more made Review.)

The lady wasn't checking spelling. She was wondering how awful a fellow's first name must be if he went by "E. Ellsworth McMeen, III."

<u>Now</u> I <u>have</u> to use my first name Elmer. Social Security and Medicare don't allow us oldsters to go by our middle names. I've now become my father, at least in appellation.

I'm not sure exactly how or when I became aware of Sheila. Although she denies this, one time she seemed unusually interested in a volume that just happened to be right above my desk, which was far away from her more exalted station as an "Editor." She was slumming in my area, maybe to check out the "Ellsworth" guy.

Sheila had graduated from Muhlenberg College Phi Beta Kappa. It wasn't enough for her simply to garner Summa Cum Laude honors; she also received her degree with Highest Honors in her major of History. (Unlike me, who had the same major, Sheila actually <u>remembers</u> events in history.) She was cute, not with some Ken-and-Barbie blandness, but character, good bones, sophisticated, nice figure, great curly dark hair, and striking blue eyes that were warm and sensitive. She dressed really well, too. Sparks were igniting, at least on my end.

I summoned the courage to ask her out, but was too chicken to do it directly. I slipped a note onto her desk. Sheila kept the note. The reason I know it's the original note is that I signed it with my last name. Sheila agreed to go out with me.

We can't remember whether Sheila came to my apartment on the first date. I do remember early on in our relationship playing guitar for her, amidst the tumbleweeds of dust, bare light bulbs, and general squalor of my apartment on Rittenhouse Square. We had a nice dinner at a good Philly Restaurant, Tarello's on Chestnut Street in Center City. We then went to the movie "Joe," starring Peter Boyle. Yikes; big mistake by me. Violence, mayhem, killing, decidedly not a date flick. I messed up on that one.

She was the warmest, smartest, and funniest girl I had ever been out with. It was much more than having a good sense of humor. Sheila was hilarious, the way she expressed herself, used her hands, talked, gesticulated, rolled her eyes. Even to this day I get a kick out of watching Sheila walk down to the corner to pick up the mail, flipping her hands and moving her legs in a certain jaunty manner that is incredibly endearing. I don't want to make her self-conscious about this, but I had to report it.

Her nickname to me at law school quickly became "Bird" or "Birdie." I can't remember exactly why. It had something to do with the little bird "Woodstock" in the "Peanuts" cartoon series. We may have camped on "Peanuts" because the character Frieda, like Sheila, had "naturally curly hair."

I found a letter to my mother, dated around that time, praising Sheila to the skies. I can therefore play lawyer and point to the existence of credible, contemporaneous, written evidence of what I write here 48 years later.

At our 40th anniversary party in 2011, I offered proof to the assembled multitude that God intended for the two of us to meet and be married. First were the circumstances of my being accepted at Penn, and how my application had been mislaid. If I hadn't gotten up the gumption to call, I would have ended up somewhere else, probably University of Chicago.

Then there was the circumstance of Law Review. In 1969 Sheila had written a paper to be considered for Review, but the paper was mislaid. Time passed, and Sheila assumed she hadn't made it. In a subsequent conversation with one of the Editors, she mentioned the submission, and found out that it had never been received or reviewed. She produced another copy. It was good enough for her admission to Review.

If Sheila hadn't been on the Review, our paths would probably never have crossed. She was living in Drexel Hill, and commuting back and forth to school. She wasn't hanging around the Goat.

But there's more. In getting my "case" ready for our 40th Anniversary dinner, I got an impression of (or heard from a still, small voice) the word "movies." That was it; "movies." Very strange. I commenced research on movies.

I started with movies in the year of my birth, 1947. What should pop up immediately but "Miracle on 34th

Street!" Where was Penn Law School? 34th Street in Philadelphia. Where did Sheila and I meet? Penn Law School. How great was that!

But there was more. If you ask Sheila even now about her favorite movie, it's "Brief Encounter," the British film starring Celia Johnson and Trevor Howard and directed by David Lean. When I looked it up in a movie book, the date associated with it in the US was Sheila's birthdate! Not just her birthday, but her actual birth <u>date</u>.

The movie proof sealed the case: Sheila and I were meant to be husband and wife.

As for personality, we were different in some ways. Sheila was quiet; I was loud, at least then. Sheila expressed affection primarily by doing really nice things for you; I was more tactile, verbalized more, and was somewhat like the sloppy dog who was licking you all the time. But we shared common values, on things like the people we liked and who was a jerk. We were both laser-beam types, focusing on our own projects for hours without a lot of talking. For example, she would be properly studying law at her apartment in Drexel Hill for the six hours I was watching football.

Sheila reads more than I do, and has a much better vocabulary. I had a bad habit in my youth of skipping words I didn't understand while reading. Moreover, Sheila tackles with ease something I cannot fathom: cryptic puzzles. I can't follow the logic of the clues for even the easiest ones.

We started dating in October 1970. We had a great time, with a lot of blatant PDOA on my part in the Review offices, at parties, and everywhere. It was sort of high-school, but she let me do it. Less than three months later, on December 31, 1970, we announced our engagement in Media, PA, at a dinner hosted by our friends Janet and Cliff Gibian. We were married at St. James Lutheran Church in Huntingdon on July 31, 1971.

Sheila, her mother Mary, and my mother managed to pull together a wedding while Sheila was studying for the New York Bar Exam, taking the Bar Review course, and then sitting for the two-day exam. Amazing. My cousin Joe Biddle loaned us a Pontiac Grand Prix for our honeymoon on Cape Cod.

23

Philly to New York

As our relationship deepened, Sheila and I had some serious logistical matters to work out. She was a third-year law student, and I a second-year. Before we met, we had accepted offers from different law firms. Clifford Alexander from Arnold & Porter in DC had interviewed me at Penn, and I had accepted an offer on the spot from him for a summer clerkship down there. Meanwhile, she had received and accepted an offer from Davis Polk & Wardwell for permanent employment in New York City. Unless something were done, I would be in my third year in Philly and Sheila would be working in the Big Apple. No way, José.

We solved it with the help of Columbia Law School. I applied to Columbia, which accepted me for my third year. Being on Law Review at Penn helped, as did our marital situation. (Oddly enough, one of the first people I saw at Columbia Law was a Penn Law classmate of mine who had done the same thing!) In granting me Honors, Penn, I found out later, simply ignored my grades at Columbia. If I had only known that earlier, I might not have worked so hard at Columbia.

As it was, my year at Columbia is kind of a blur. I do remember walking out of the Federal Courts course one time. It was taught by a famous scholar Professor Herbert

Wechsler, but it was a cold, winter's day and there was no heat in the classroom.

I believe the Lord protected me in all kinds of situations in Philly and later New York. After all, I was basically a rural kid trying to operate in two of the great cities of our country. After dates with Sheila in Philly, for example, I would take the subway back to Center City at all hours, as late as 1 AM. Not all the passengers on the train at that hour were friendly or sober. Sheila loaned me her VW Beetle more than once, and I would be driving it in Philly in snowstorms, or in parts of Philly where, to paraphrase Bruce Springsteen's song "Johnny 99," the light turns red and you don't stop.

On this subject, one time in my apartment after a date with Sheila, I was messing with the curtain rod, and the whole thing came down, point first, and hit me within an eighth-inch of my right eyeball. Even though wearing an eye patch might make one stand out in a crowd, I'd rather have the eye, thank you, Lord.

I almost forgot another near-crisis. When we were living in Brooklyn and driving on the Brooklyn-Queens Expressway in the VW Beetle, we got hit by a truck and spun completely around on a metal plate in the road. If we had flipped over, I wouldn't be here to write this. Instead, the car ended up pointing in the very direction we were going! Sheila and I were a bit rattled, but we had tennis time reserved out on Long Island and didn't want to lose it. We sallied forth. Oh, to be young and oblivious again.

24

NYC

If you want to read a great description of New York City, pick up E.B. White's little book called <u>Here is New York</u> (Curtis, 1949). It is somewhat outdated, having been written in 1949, but it's brilliant, discerning, and funny.

To me, however, NYC was huge, basically unmanageable, and full of ear-splitting subway and traffic noise. There were also way too many bicyclists going the wrong way on one-way streets, hoping you'd hit them so they could sue you. Moreover, if three drops of rain fell in Manhattan, everything would come to a grinding halt. OK, I'm being melodramatic, but tell me I'm wrong.

I would have been happy to stay in Philly and practice law there at one of the big firms. I liked the scale of Philly, the grid pattern, and the availability of concerts and great music at Curtis Institute, without having to expend a lot of effort to get there. It was manageable; you could actually drive in Philly without risking life and limb. I didn't bond with the Eagles or the Flyers, mind you, but it had Big Five college basketball, and the Palestra arena was at Penn.

Philly was not to be. After our month of married life in DC while I finished up my clerkship at Arnold & Porter, Sheila and I headed to New York.

She and I had separately been to the City many times in our early years. My mother would take me to Broadway shows every now and then, traveling from Lewistown or Huntingdon. We'd stay at hotels where we had "due bills," meaning that the hotel owed our newspaper money for advertising, and we would take it out "in trade" by staying there.

Sometimes the hotels weren't the best, or in the best neighborhoods. I noticed some scantily-clad ladies outside the Hotel Astor one time who seemed very available for dates. On one whirlwind visit to New York, Mother and I did two fantastic shows in the same day: "Fiddler on the Roof" and "Man of La Mancha." That's a <u>lot</u> of Broadway for one day.

Even with that experience, I was still a boy from the sticks and my approach to New York was amazingly naïve. We thought about living in Manhattan, but I didn't think I could handle the pace and noise. In addition, I wasn't sure how we could be certain to get a parking place in front of an apartment building to unload our stuff in a move. Really; I actually worried about that.

Then there was the incident with the moving truck. We had decided to live in Brooklyn Heights. It was a relatively quiet residential area, one subway stop from Wall Street and Sheila's firm. We rented a U-Haul truck in Huntingdon, looked at a map for the closest drop-off location for the truck in Brooklyn, and were on our way.

The move into the six-floor apartment building on Grace Court went well. The street was a tree-lined cul-de-sac, and the stately Grace episcopal church stood across from the building. Sheila and I unloaded, and my sister Franny guarded the truck. I can see dear Franny even now, sitting in the truck and consuming an ice cream cone purchased from a passing vendor.

The next day Sheila and I set out to return the truck. The drop-off location was on Fulton Street in Brooklyn, and the address had a lot of numbers in it. We knew where Fulton Street started, so we went there and figured to drive a little way and dump the truck. Well, we drove, and drove, and drove; the neighborhoods got worse, and worse, and worse. Finally, in the middle of "Bed-Stuy" (the Bedford-Stuyvesant section of Brooklyn) we found the dilapidated garage for our drop-off. The owner was quite grateful to receive the truck; even amazed. He couldn't recall <u>ever</u> having a rental truck returned to his garage in that area of Brooklyn.

Digs in Brooklyn.

25

Brooklyn

If we had to do it over again, we would have tried Manhattan. I would have found some way to allay my fear that a parking place wouldn't be available when we wanted to move.

The Heights area was quiet, necessities were available without a lot of effort, and there were nice places to walk. The Promenade overlooked the East River and provided a magnificent view of lower Manhattan. I discovered Chinese food in the Heights. My friends who grew up in New York were amazed that I was 24 before ever having eaten Chinese food, even on Christmas.

The problem was that most of the music and arts in the city were in Manhattan. To get there and back, you had to ride the noisy, crowded subway, which was a downer especially after some uplifting performance by the Metropolitan or City Opera. From "Carmen" to Court Street Station; from "Turandot" to Times Square Station. I'll stop now.

Our one-bedroom apartment on Grace Court was spacious and comfortable, and didn't face an air shaft. I have some ancient and unduly dark moving pictures of friends who visited us there. The elevators worked, and all was good for a while.

Then we acquired some new neighbors, two young girls. They may have been students somewhere. They were not very tidy. Moreover, they apparently had failed to pay their electric bill because for weeks on end an electric cord from their apartment ran from under their door into a socket in the hall.

After a while, critters started to show up in our apartment. The girls and their habits were the culprits. Cockroaches are part of the lore of NYC, but why did they have to be so happily drawn to our apartment? You'd drop some food on the floor, and five of them with knives and forks would rush out from under the fridge. It got so bad that we would have people visiting, and three inches behind them on the wall a critter would be strolling as if he owned the place. I guess he did.

We finally had to leave. The roaches had won. The building was nice, and I'm sure still is. I suspect that the roach problem left with those girls.

We moved two blocks away, to a third-floor walkup apartment in a brownstone on Joralemon Street. We lived there for another two years, suffering through the winter months when the place was cold and I was writing angry letters to the landlord. The real problem was that the heat control for the whole building was in the ground-floor apartment, and the people there liked it cool. Feeling more and more claustrophobic in the city environment, we youngsters in 1975 moved to northern New Jersey in an area of the state where Sheila grew up, with her parents and brother Paul.

We would be home-owners, debtors to the "man," and tax-paying residents of the beautiful little community of Mountain Lakes, NJ. Before getting into houses, let's go back to music for a bit.

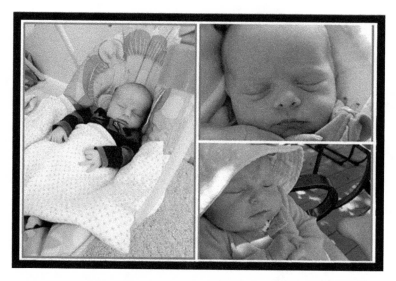

Clockwise from Left: Conner J. McMeen, Evelyn H. Kohan, and Kelsey M. McMeen, as babies in repose. The grandchildren rate a picture, even if it <u>is</u> out of sequence in the book.

26

Music; Plateau

Guitar-playing took a back seat in the early years of our life in NY/NJ. I had plateaued, or maybe I was treading water. Some mildly pejorative metaphor applied.

I asked Sheila once what I was playing then; I couldn't remember. Her answer was honest but not completely informative: "Whatever you were playing in the 1960's." I was singing and picking then, so I guess that's what I was doing in the 1970's and early 1980's. Mid-1980's began another music period that was important, and I'll cover that later.

I do have cassette copies of radio shows I did with my mother in Huntingdon, where I sang and played, as well as some home recording I did for her in the 1970's. I also have a recording of a set I played at a 1974 summer arts festival in Huntingdon. I think it's pretty darned good, especially since my mother had given me short notice of it. ("Sandy, do you want to play at the Huntingdon County Arts Festival?" "Sure; when is it?" "Oh, it's tomorrow.") I shouldn't blame her; I think someone dropped out at the last minute and she suggested me to the powers-that-be.

I did so-called "alternating-bass fingerpicking," of a type generally associated with Chet Atkins, but not even close to his level of skill and artistry. I sang folk tunes and pop tunes -- Glen Campbell, Gordon Lightfoot. I loved

Lightfoot's monster song "Canadian Railroad Trilogy," which I did on a 12-string at the 1974 arts festival. That song has some tricky strumming. Gordon made it look easy, but it wasn't. I like the sound of my voice at that arts festival; the cigarettes in my youth hadn't ruined it. Mother was unhappy, however, claiming that I wasn't close enough to the mic when I sang (even though the recording guys said I was).

I do remember Don McLean's great song "American Pie," and trying to figure out all the pop references. It was too long to learn, as was "Alice's Restaurant" by Arlo Guthrie.

All of this is by way of saying there wasn't a lot of breaking news back then on the El music front.

There was, however, an earlier event that was promising. I had a singing (and dating) partner in the late 1960's, Beth Shaffer. Beth and I won some awards as a duo, performing in central PA. I recall that we sang Steve Gillette's song "Back on the Street Again." We won a contest at the "Shade Gap Picnic" in 1968, which was more important than the name might imply. We were selected to compete in a statewide talent contest in Harrisburg, and came in second. The winner was a little girl who wore a pretty pink dress and danced. We were robbed, but she was cuter than we were, I guess. OK, sour grapes alert.

I discovered years later that the Shade Gap contest took place almost exactly three years before Sheila and my wedding date.

27

Mountain Lakes, NJ

In January 1975, on a cold but sunny day, Sheila and I
drove the VW out to a town called Mountain Lakes in
Morris County, NJ, never to return to New York. That's
dramatic but a bit inaccurate: Sheila was to work five more
years at Davis Polk, and I was to work 25 more years in
Manhattan. But as far as living in the City, Sheila and I
were gone-zo.

Mountain Lakes was a "bedroom community" of about
4,000 souls, surrounding a small lake. It was incorporated
in 1924, and many of the so-called "Laker" houses were of
that vintage. According to something I read, the vast
majority of adults in the town had at least a Bachelor's
degree in college, quadruple the national average. It had a
lake section and hill section. Its school system had a stellar
reputation in the state. For a school that size, it also had a
darned good football team from year to year. A
walking/riding path bordered the main drag in town, called
"The Boulevard." If you wanted to shop or buy any serious
quantity of groceries, however, you had to go to nearby
Denville, or to Boonton, where Sheila grew up.

We had a great address in Mountain Lakes: 30 Oak
Lane. It was simple, and you didn't have to spell it for
anybody. (I contrast that with our address in Huntingdon
beginning in late 2012, which was "Arbor Bluff Drive," a
mouthful.) "30 Oak Lane," moreover, sounded like

something straight out of Mayberry and the old Andy Griffith show. I'm dating myself.

The house had four official bedrooms, but really five counting the third floor. It was old, built in the early days of the town, but in good shape. It had white stucco on the outside, and beautiful chestnut paneling (or "wainscoting") on the inside. It was a lot of house for us two kids who had lived in a walk-up apartment in Brooklyn the day before. We rattled around in it, harboring thoughts of populating it with little McMeens at some point. The house had property in the back, and almost a full building lot on the side. It also had a garage.

We were to live in that house for nearly 28 years, almost a generation. You might think that a Chapter on Mountain Lakes would go on and on (reminding me of the joke about the fictional rehab program for compulsive talkers called "On-and-on Anon"). The opposite is true. The temptation for me is to make it too short.

My wife and kids could write volumes on Mountain Lakes, but my vocational world was in the City. I would get up at 5-6 AM, eat breakfast, play a little guitar, catch the train or bus to New York, and on a good day get back home at 7:45 PM. Weekday fun-time in Mountain Lakes was decidedly limited. That fact was not lost on our children, none of whom has chosen a New-York-commuter career path. Sheila on the other hand could write pages about the excellent schools in town (she was on the School Board for eight years), the Community Church (she was a trustee), all kinds of episodes involving our four kids, their activities, schooling, and occasional run-ins with the law. A lot of it, I must confess, is a blur to me.

I assure you, however, that I was not a Bad-Dad-Who-Can't-Remember-His-Kids'-Childhood-and-Therefore-Is-a-Jerk. When we sold the house in 2003, the new owners did a massive rehab and update job on the house, and the original footprint disappeared. Sheila and I would occasionally drive past the house during a subsequent trip through town, but the house we had lived in didn't really exist anymore. Staring at the old homestead, musing about the good, old days, wasn't a possibility. The kids feel the same way.

I actually <u>could</u> write a lot about Mountain Lakes, but this book has an important spiritual theme and I don't want to get sidetracked. There are some amusing stories I must share, however.

The day after we moved in, something happened that made me almost jump out of my skin. The doorbell rang. I kid you not. I thought our house was being invaded. During our two years in the third-floor walkup in Brooklyn, hardly anyone <u>ever</u> came to our door. I know this sounds crazy, but it took me months to get used to friendly neighbors ringing the doorbell, to hang out or bring us nice flowers or candy. I wasn't paranoid, nor were "they" after me. I just had to get used to the rhythm of living in civilized society after 4-1/2 years in New York City.

Another feature of our life at 30 Oak Lane was that it had no first-floor bathroom. There were two on the second-floor, so you always had to go upstairs to "go." Our kids' generation today would consider that outrageous and third-world. But that's how a lot of the so-called "Laker Houses" were built. In the 1980's we did a major house rehab, and had a little half-bath tucked in between the first floor and basement.

The house had some shag carpeting that we discovered later had been seriously desecrated by the dog of some prior owner. But the house also had something I loved – a plaid red carpet in the kitchen. It was wild and colorful. I'm not sure Sheila ever liked it, and it went the way of the dodo bird during the rehab of the 1980's. I still remember playing with our kids on that carpet.

The population of the house increased on May 25, 1977, on a sunny and warm day at St. Clare's Hospital in Denville, NJ. Baby Jonathan Ellsworth McMeen made an appearance. As soon as Jon came home, my beloved study at the house disappeared, being replaced by Jon and crib. That was OK; we grabbed some of the room back when we did our big rehab in the 1980's.

There was a serious God-at-work moment during Jon's gestation. In the late stages of Sheila's pregnancy, we were returning home from work in the city on the NJ Transit Boonton-Line train. We were traveling at a decent rate of speed through the meadowlands near Secaucus in an area where there was a significant drop on both sides of the track. As we were rolling along, the train derailed. We passengers were bouncing up and down on our seats, items were falling off the overhead racks, and it was all pretty hairy. The train clattered along the roadbed for hundreds of feet before coming to a stop. That was close.

Daniel Biddle McMeen arrived on March 9, 1980, two days after my co-author John Sarchio, Esq. and I wrote a giant article on an obscure point of aviation law for "The Journal of Air Law and Commerce." Dan turned out to be much more interesting, and more fun, than our seminal contribution to the legal literature.

Dan did throw some scares into us, jumping off the roof at the elementary school for some yet unexplained reason, nearly cutting off his thumb in shop class at the school, and having some other "legal issues." We'll get into those later.

Very early on in Dan's life, <u>he</u> was the beneficiary of a God-at-work moment. When Dan was a baby, Sheila and I were at a meeting in town when our housekeeper called and said that a tree had fallen down in our yard. That was true, but there was a <u>lot</u> more to the story.

A triple-trunk oak tree next to our house, just a few feet from baby Dan's bedroom, had earlier been making creaking sounds at the base. We had it checked, and it had been pronounced healthy. It wasn't. It was rotted inside at the base. It fell down, all 50 or so feet of it, in our driveway. If we had been on the front steps, we would be deceased. If we had been in our Chevy parked in the driveway, also RIP. Lying on its side in our driveway, the trunk of that tree was higher than our VW.

As we collected ourselves the next morning and assessed the situation, we noticed some fascinating details. The tree had fallen in almost the only place that didn't harm the house, including Dan's room, or the garage. The limbs of the tree nearest the house ended up flush against the house and windows, but no windows were broken or even cracked. The top limbs of the tree had just grazed the garage, almost surgically removing the basketball hoop that had been there. The trees to the right of the driveway were not damaged.

Two kids represented a nice, even number. Sheila and I pondered whether or not we should go for three. We said why not; the first two items seemed good. We didn't count on twins. In October 1982 we discovered that Sheila was having twins. Sheila got pretty large, and I had one panic attack, but everything went well. In late January 1983 12+ pounds of baby, in the persons of James Cunningham McMeen and Mary Josephine McMeen, emerged, surrounded by a phalanx of medical people at St. Clare's. Mothers with twins received a <u>lot</u> of attention at St. Clare's.

Jimmy was born first. Five minutes later, Mary arrived, feet first. The nurse looked at Sheila and declared, "Mrs. McMeen, you got your girl!"

I probably shouldn't mention this, but the medical folks were fascinated by the fused placenta. Their handling of it reminded me for some reason of a cook at a pizza shop kneading the dough before twirling it in the air. They didn't twirl it, but I wonder whether they were tempted.

Any subject in this Chapter after the birth of our kids would be anti-climactic. Let's jump back to the Big Apple and the wonderful world of lawyers. We'll return to Mountain Lakes later.

28

Cravath, Swaine & Moore, Esquires

Sheila was a litigation Associate attorney at Davis Polk. I interviewed with Davis Polk, and really liked the people there. It was "white shoe," but not stuffy, and there were Penn people there, including the Partner who interviewed me, Sam Pryor. Sam was the genuine article, but it simply was better for Sheila and me to be at different firms.

Three venerable and internationally respected law firms in Manhattan were Davis Polk, Cravath, Swaine & Moore, and Sullivan & Cromwell. They all did big-ticket Corporate and Litigation work, attracted top law students, and paid good money. The hours would be long and the work demanding, but I didn't see any immediate alternative.

I interviewed with Sullivan & Cromwell, but the fit wasn't right for me. A fine gentleman, Penn Law graduate, and Partner there Mitchell Brock made a special effort and reached out to me after I took myself out of the running. I appreciated that, but I was a kid from rural PA, and felt it was just too buttoned-down and Wall Street for me.

Cravath was different. To be sure, the firm was loaded with people from Harvard Law and Yale Law. I felt a little like a second-class citizen coming from Penn (even though Penn is routinely listed among the top ten law schools in the country). My anxiety quickly evaporated after my first interview. Ralph McAfee, a litigation Partner and big, outgoing Texan, took a liking to me. We really hit it off. Maybe it was a Texas-PA thing. At the conclusion of the interview, I noticed a small sheet of paper in front of him with a lot of blank boxes under headings A through D. With a flourish, he checked all the "A" boxes in front of me, and passed the sheet along to the secretary who was taking me around. I had a few other interviews, got an offer, accepted it with alacrity, and started work on September 5, 1972.

I had no idea of whether I'd be any good as a lawyer. You could be a good law student and not cut it in law practice. At Cravath new Associates had to choose their area of practice from the get-go, rather than dabbling in different areas for a year and then choosing. I don't know whether they still do that.

I chose Corporate, not because I knew anything about it, but because I was concerned about my physical ability to function as a lawyer in a courtroom setting, standing up, questioning witnesses, and thinking on my feet. I found out later that big-firm litigators might spend huge chunks of their career without ever conducting a trial or seeing the inside of a courtroom other than an appellate court. In a Corporate deal I figured we'd all sit around a table and squabble about deal points. I wasn't far wrong.

At Cravath, people were a bit formal. Partners were addressed as Mr. or, in the rare case then, Mrs. (I recall only one female Partner back then.) A yawning professional and social chasm existed between us Associates and the Partners. It was hard to make Partner at Cravath, and a little respect was considered their due. Memos would go out to "Partners and Staff."

Cravath had a great name in the law biz, and being an Associate there got you props among your peers in New York and elsewhere. Technically, I wasn't even a lawyer. I had to pass the Bar Exam, have the results announced, meet the character and fitness requirements, and be formally admitted to the New York State Bar. All of that did not come together until February of 1973. (Sheila and I did pass the Bar on the first try.) I was in effect a legal assistant, but people didn't really obsess on such fine points. The Partners ran the show and everyone knew it.

For my three years at Cravath, Sheila and I worked in the same building, One Chase Manhattan Plaza, downtown Manhattan and a few streets north of the real "Wall Street." It was fun for us. We could commute together, and go out to lunch together at various places, including "The Market" in the World Trade Center, which was only a couple of blocks from One Chase.

One time we were together near the Trade Center when they were filming the re-make of "King Kong." We observed a huge brown heap of something on the sidewalk, which represented King Kong after his demise. Of course, the attacks of 9/11, and the hideous loss of life, cast a pall over just about any story involving the Trade Center.

I had two assignments at Cravath during my short tenure there. My first was with Partner Henry ("Harry") Riordan, an expert on railroad financing who also handled public offerings of securities for various investment banking firms.

Shortly after I arrived I was tasked to a tech company north of Atlanta. Cravath's client was the proposed "underwriter" for the upcoming offering of securities by the tech company. An "underwriter" is an investment firm that contracts, under specified conditions in the "underwriting agreement," to buy the securities offered by the issuing corporation and re·sell them to the public. I was to do "due diligence" on the minute books of the tech company.

I was diligent, but quite undue, because I took way more time than anticipated, didn't quite know what I was doing, and nearly ran out of money down there. I later picked up on the "drill" in reviewing corporate minutes. We newbies were to confirm that sufficient corporate authorization existed for the deal, and to ascertain whether there were any "red flags" raising issues that should be disclosed in the prospectus and other filings with the Securities and Exchange Commission ("SEC").

Later on, as a six·month Associate, I got involved in a situation that was very dicey. Cravath had developed a model of underwriting agreement for one of its underwriting clients. It contained recommended provisions and was even footnoted. After sending it over to the client underwriter, who should walk in the door but a company client of Cravath's that wanted to do a deal with that very underwriter. Let's call the company issuing the securities "D" company, and the underwriter "S" company. Because there was a conflict, the underwriter S company retained another law firm to represent it in the deal. That law firm was LeBoeuf, Lamb, Leiby & MacRae. I would come to know it well.

Usually in public offerings there isn't much fussing about the underwriting agreement. In this case, however, D didn't like some provisions of the Cravath model.

We all were at the printer surrounded by stacks of documents waiting to be filed with the SEC. D didn't like the "market out" provision of the underwriting agreement. That term allowed the underwriter to defer the deal if the underwriter didn't like the market at the time. D thought that was too much discretion in the underwriter and wanted to impose a "reasonableness" standard. Under D's proposal, the underwriter could dump the deal only if it "reasonably" thought the market conditions were bad. The underwriter S was worried about being second-guessed later if it had to defer the deal.

The Cravath Senior Associate and I, the exceedingly junior one, sat at the printer while the principals argued the point <u>all night long</u>. At about 6 in the morning, it hit me that D wasn't really talking about an objective standard like "reasonableness" but instead simple "honesty." The latter concept is captured by the phrase "in good faith."

I walked over to the LeBoeuf Partner and wrote in the margin of his draft the words "in good faith." I then hit the men's room, after being overdue for about six hours.

When I returned, the deal was done using the phrase "in good faith!" I think that everyone was tired and just wanted some language to make the problem go away. But I must say this: decades later I believe I got a "word" from the Lord saying that it was <u>He</u> who had given me the solution to show how important "faith" is! I told you He has a great sense of humor.

147

For a newbie lawyer, being involved in solving a problem was a real shot in the arm. But there were all kinds of other consequences for me. Two years later one of the lawyers at LeBoeuf called me and asked whether I would consider leaving Cravath and moving to LeBoeuf. After a lot of soul-searching on my part, lists of pro's and con's, and further discussions, and receiving assurances regarding the Partnership track at LeBoeuf, I accepted the offer.

There's more. D company decided to use LeBoeuf as its counsel in future financings. Years later when I was at LeBoeuf, who should poke his head into my office but the Treasurer of D company. The first words out of his mouth, before even saying "hello," were "in good faith!" The words were still in their form of underwriting agreement!

Before getting into LeBoeuf, and my 25 years there, I need to share more about Cravath. I must do justice to that great firm. My experience there was critical to my own development as a lawyer. The firm had high standards and provided assignments that led me to discover my own style, interests, and, hopefully, strengths.

My second assignment was working for Partner Allen Merrill, a Yale Law graduate and distinguished southern gentleman who hailed from Alabama. He spoke slowly and well, with exhalations of cigarette smoke at the correct spots in every well-crafted sentence. The shades in his office were always drawn, giving the place an eerily subdued (some might say funereal) atmosphere. I did hear later that Allen liked to write poetry in French and read the poems to his wife under a tree at his country home upstate. I don't remember the source, but that sounded romantic.

Mr. Merrill's primary practice involved representation of banks as "corporate trustee" in debt financings. His main client was Chemical Bank in New York. Chemical's primary lawyer for its sexier banking business was another Cravath Partner Dick Simmons, one of the premier banking lawyers in the city and the bank's chief outside counsel. Chemical made serious money in the lending area, and much less in the corporate trust area. The Associates at the firm considered the corporate trust assignment to be somewhat of a backwater, but the work was very important to Merrill. He delegated the deals almost completely to the Associate and expected the Associate to do them and come to him only with problems. That turned out to be perfect for me.

A company desiring to issue public debt securities, like bonds or debentures, would contract with the bank, as trustee, as required by the federal Trust Indenture Act of 1939. That law established mandatory terms for the document, called a trust indenture. Additionally, the indenture would contain specific covenants for the protection of the holders of the securities, default clauses, and remedies that the trustee would pursue in protection of the holders.

I got to be very friendly with the bank officers in Chemical's corporate trust department. They tended to feel oppressed by the atmosphere of hard work and low fees, and the regular pressure on them by the bank's customer-relationship people to read complicated documents fast and not have any comments.

I would go over there often to discuss various indentures with them. They liked my genuine enthusiasm. They themselves were among the most detail-oriented businessmen I have ever dealt with. You couldn't be a broad-brush guy and be any good at corporate trust; there were too many traps for the unwary. Our worst fear was that an indenture might contain some ambiguity that would make the trustee's life miserable down the road in default situations, or in squabbling with accountants on what financial terms meant, or, God forbid, in setting the interest rate for variable-rate securities. The trustee was always permitted to receive and rely on legal opinions, but the bank wanted to avoid if at all possible crises down the road that sucked up time, energy, and money.

With one major exception, I didn't have to draft whole documents, but I did review a <u>lot</u> of paper. It was great experience for me to see many examples of the work product of fine law firms, compare them for strengths and possible weaknesses, and along the way develop my own preferences for wording. I even pounced on the so-called "boilerplate" language at the end of the document. Gremlins could show up in that area, since the eyes of the draftsman of the document might well have glazed over by the time he or she hit that part. I happily wallowed in the subtle differences among the different models.

After a while I may have developed a reputation as being fussier than good trustee's counsel should be. The other parties just wanted the trustee to bless the document, sign it, and be happy with the modest fee it would receive. I, on the other hand, tended to see possible problems under every rock, and wanted to fix them. In the process, I was developing a certain style in negotiations, with an intuition on when to haggle on a point and when to defer it to later discussion after, hopefully, my bona fides had been established. For example, if you as trustee's counsel recommend that the words "to and including" be changed to the word "to," and thereby save an issuer thousands of dollars in interest, you achieve some credibility with its chief financial officer. That happened once.

I represented another bank as trustee in the first big floating-rate note deal. I was completely obsessive about the indenture being clear on the interest rate under all possible circumstances, including the Rapture and Armageddon. The trustee simply wasn't being paid enough to be in the middle of any war on the interest rate, in a deal for $650,000,000, which wasn't chump change in 1974. The lawyers for the issuer didn't mock my agita; they appreciated the effort, and the result was a good indenture.

It was unusual for trustee's counsel to receive as a trophy a "bound volume" of the deal papers, since our role was typically considered to be a necessary annoyance, or an annoying necessity, but they gave me one. It graces my shelf to this day, having survived several moves.

One of the hardest deals I did as a young Associate involved corporate trust. Chemical Bank was trustee in the first commercial-paper trust financing, done as a private placement, for the construction of a major facility. A private placement was a transaction that involved a limited number of purchasers of the securities and therefore wasn't a public offering subject to the filing and other formalities of the SEC.

The company was an oil company, and the plant was in Texas. I could write a whole book on that deal. It was novel and required writing contracts from scratch. The Associate at Sullivan & Cromwell and I worked on documents for days and weeks. During one month I had 360 billable hours, almost unheard of in the history of Associate hours in New York.

Interestingly enough, the Associate Frank Rykowski was married to Jane on the same day in 1971 as Sheila and I were. He didn't have the honor of having his wedding covered in the Huntingdon Daily News; he had to settle for the New York Times.

We did an all-nighter before the target closing date, Friday, July 26, 1974, but the deal blew amidst a potpourri of problems and recriminations. I remember Chemical's special Texas counsel Bill Joor, from the prominent Houston firm Vinson & Elkins, standing at the door of Chemical's office witnessing the chaos, and saying over and over, "This is crazy, this is crazy."

Bill and I went out to dinner at Harry's at Hanover Square and reviewed the wreckage. I didn't generally drink much, as you might expect from my family history. The five Bacardi cocktails I consumed that night definitely exceeded my limit. It was only with difficulty that I found my way back to One Chase that night.

The deal got back on track and closed on August 2. I got a bound volume on that one, too; Frank made sure of it.

Allen Merrill himself remembered the insane amount of work I had done on that deal. I was blessed that he mentioned it at a retirement lunch thrown for him in 1980 or so, years after I had left the firm.

29

Mountain Lakes Redux

Having tested your patience on minutiae of law practice, let's go back to Mountain Lakes for a bit.

When I told son Jon about writing my memoirs, he said, "I assume you'll cover the Mountain Lakes police station." I had actually forgotten about that, but not anymore.

There was a period in our life in Mountain Lakes during which it seemed I was getting calls from the neighbors or police every two minutes. It really wasn't that bad, but I was under pressure at work and any ripples in the usually calm waters at home created agita. Sheila protected me from the vast majority of issues. Unlike the spouses of some of my law colleagues, Sheila didn't call me four or five times a day to discuss where we should go out to eat that weekend or how to contact the phone repairman. Even when Dan nearly cut his thumb off in shop class she didn't call me until the situation had been stabilized.

There were matters, however, that occurred when I was home and couldn't escape. A friend called one time to inquire why Jon was in the vicinity of the elementary school at four in the morning. I still don't know why; he probably doesn't either. On one Halloween, the police accused the same Jon of listening to police activities on a scanner and alerting his miscreant friends to police whereabouts. He has denied that, at least to date. As for Dan, he once goaded

Jimmy into ringing the neighbor's doorbell and running away, and the neighbor Howard called us about that.

Dan himself would be involved in a driving incident, with, shall we say, some culpability, necessitating my arising from a deep and well-earned sleep to "visit" with the police at the station in Mountain Lakes. The kids recall with glee my language when the latter happened. I told them that I've since repented and really try not to take the Lord's name in vain.

Mary had an incident while driving the car in Denville, grazing a kid on a bike. She said it was his fault. (I always thought Mary could have been a lawyer, just like her three brothers.) When we called the parents of the kid to apologize, the father seemed madder at the kid than he was at Mary. Maybe it <u>was</u> the kid's fault.

Back to Dan. He played guitar in a rock group with a name that was printable, but barely. They did gigs in various places, including New York City. Around Thanksgiving one year, Dan came up to me and confessed that he had been nabbed on the streets of New York with an open can of an adult beverage. The problem was twofold: the container was open and he was not an adult. He informed me that the hearing was the next day.

I berated him, of course, in part because my upcoming work week was going to be intense. The maximum penalty was a fine of $25, and I thought briefly about just letting the thing go. But then I thought, presciently it turns out, "Dan might be a lawyer one day, and I don't want this on his record."

The next day Dan went to school and I went to court in New York as his counsel. I had just spent a bunch of money on some Paul Stuart suits, and for the first time I had a suit on that actually fit me around the shoulders. (If you want to see a guy with suits that fit, check out Prince Charles.) Anyway, I went down to the municipal court on Centre Street and joined the line for the court session. It was an interesting group of people, to say the least, who looked at me as if I were from a different planet.

I entered the courtroom and approached the clerk. He looked me up and down and said, "You don't get down here much, do you?" We both had a good laugh, and I engaged in a minor rant against Dan. I was prepared to plead guilty, pay the fine, and get out. He got the ticket, looked at it, and sotta voce said, "The officer didn't sign the ticket. It's invalid and the case will be dismissed."

Dan's name was called and I stepped up. The judge was a lady. She took one look at me, and I knew she hated me. "Where's the Defendant?" she demanded. "He's in school in New Jersey, Your Honor. I'm his father and I represent him." She scowled at me. The clerk handed her the ticket and a short discussion ensued. "Case dismissed!" she declared through gritted teeth. I thanked her, glanced at the clerk with appreciation, and left the courtroom. I wasn't cut out to be a litigator, but I was looking good in that suit.

Talking about looking good, Sheila and I have been blessed with great children. My temptation is to launch into a full-blown hagiography on each of them. They are all compassionate, and none of them has a mean bone in his or her body. They seem to like each other these days, too.

I started to compose descriptions of each one, but it's impossible. If I write too little, it's unfair to them and I'll feel guilty. If I go on for pages, I'll embarrass them. And what about their wonderful spouses? And what about the three "perfect" grand-children? Even their pets are pretty nice. I just don't want you to think that I've neglected our children in favor of indulging in guitar trivia.

I can say that the traveling McMeen Sextet always created a stir wherever we went, whether it was crowding into a booth at Chili's or boarding an airplane flight. We took the kids on vacations to Arizona, West Virginia, Florida, Maine, and the Poconos, among other places. Three times Jimmy flew to Europe for soccer tournaments in which his club team, the Chatham (NJ) Cobras, participated. Mary was an avid dancer for many years, and Sheila drove her all over the map to dance competitions and performances. Mary was also President of her Sorority at St. Lawrence University, and I'm really proud of her for taking on that responsibility, and for many other reasons. She has a senior position in the educational field now, and is a great mother, to boot.

Dan is the kind of guy who is a sociable fellow, but you suspect that behind closed doors he's hitting the books and grinding things out. He graduated with Honors from college and law school. He also is quite musical. I still have a cassette tape somewhere of his playing on the piano at a school function the first part of Scott Joplin's "The Entertainer." He's a guitarist, too, as well as a Partner in a law firm.

Jimmy is Mr. Laser-Beam, with amazing powers of concentration and a great academic record in high school, college, and law school, as well as accomplishments as a lawyer. He's a great dad, too, of Conner and Kelsey.

Jon, our oldest, has amazing skill sets from fixing things, to landscaping, to law practice, to serving as a municipal prosecutor. Supposedly he looks and talks like me, so he's blessed. Hahaha. He has my sense of humor, so he should like this book.

We had some adventures as a family. We were all on a plane flying southwest out of Denver one time, and hit massive turbulence. It was pretty terrifying. [Note from El: You might want to fly to Phoenix through Dallas rather than through Denver.] The kids were so scared they all fell asleep. That wind coming East over the Rockies is not cool, when you are flying into it sometimes. There was a flavor of "game over" for the McMeen tribe there for awhile.

We had another adventure at a resort in Maine in the summer of 1991. We had to evacuate thanks to Hurricane Bob. The six of us were hustled off to a gymnasium somewhere in Maine, off the coast. While Sheila and I were wondering whether the gym roof would blow off, the kids were enjoying the Chinese food the Red Cross provided. (Chinese food; not exactly the native cuisine of Maine, we thought, but it <u>was</u> good!)

The McMeen kids could be lucky, too. Jon and some others arrived a little late one night before Jimmy's college graduation in 2005. In an odd turn of events, they were assigned the Presidential Suite at the Charles Hotel in Cambridge, Mass. You might say, what's the big deal? It was dumb luck. It's interesting, however, that the former Vice President of the United States, one Mr. Al Gore, was in the hotel that very night. He was there to attend the graduation of his son, and got stuck with a modest room like ours. A gaggle of McMeen kids somehow aced out the former VP.

30

Spiritual Intermission II: Was God in NJ and NY?

To answer the question in the Chapter title, He certainly was, as indicated or intimated earlier. But I didn't have a personal relationship with Him.

He was in the law practice, He was in Mountain Lakes, He was in the situations involving Dan, protecting him against the massive tree that fell down, and protecting him against risk-taking in future years with driving and alcohol. Dan was nabbed one block from our house in an incident with alcohol. If he had gotten away with it, he might well have continued on a path of risk-taking that was perilous.

I have discussed with our children the fact that I was not spiritually mature during most of their youth. As a result, I've had to play catch-up with them on the gospel of Jesus Christ. Put another way, I delegated to the Community Church of Mountain Lakes the responsibility. That wasn't right, not because the church did anything wrong but because the gospel has to be taught at home and reinforced through prayer and regular reading and discussion of the Scriptures. As a result, the kids had to go through their early lives with our ethical teachings and model, to be sure, but without knowledge of the supernatural power of God operating through the Holy Spirit and available to believers through faith.

I recognize that children do not tell you all that's on their minds. Their thoughts as youngsters and teenagers may be more in the nature of impressions than fully formed assessments. I say this to allow for the possibility that the situation was better than I am positing here. The kids may well have been closer to the Lord than I knew at the time. Maybe even I was.

In any event, matters on the fronts of family, law, music, and God were to accelerate and begin to converge after I went to LeBoeuf, Lamb, Leiby & MacRae. Let's go down to LeBoeuf, at 140 Broadway, across the plaza from One Chase.

31

Cravats, and Beef and Lamb

It's really immature of me to give a title to this Chapter that is a play on words for the fine law firms Cravath, Swaine & Moore and LeBoeuf, Lamb, Leiby & MacRae. I suggested earlier that my sense of humor may be regressing. It may simply have stalled at age 13.

On August 8, 1975, I left Cravath. It was an auspicious day, if not date: Richard Nixon had announced his resignation as President the year before on that very date. No scandal precipitated my leaving, at least to my knowledge.

Shortly before I left Cravath, an interesting piece of street theater took place in its hallowed halls. The Partner at Cravath to whom I had been assigned saw me in the hall and asked when I could start working for him. I said I was leaving the firm. He stared at me for a few moments and then walked away, showing a significant amount of disinterest in my career trajectory. He was beleaguered with clients demanding his very dedicated and excellent services, so in later years I cut him some slack. Back then, however, it seemed odd. Actually, I'm wrong; what was odd was that it <u>didn't</u> seem odd at the time. It only seemed odd <u>after</u> I was at LeBoeuf for a while, shared the story, and saw stunned looks on the faces of the people there.

I joined LeBoeuf on August 18. It was then a firm of about 70, while Cravath was bigger, at 125. I hadn't goofed off those ten days. I knew that LeBoeuf wanted me to work on deals, so I pored over some papers on a Cravath deal trying to get up to speed on the art and skill of lease financing. I spent hours at my trestle desk at home, reading through and making notations on opaque sets of papers. I discovered later to my great dismay that the papers I was studying reflected some eccentricities of Texas law, and that their applicability to other transactions might well be quite limited. I was toiling in my beloved study from which I would be evicted in May 1977 by baby Jon and his crib.

My first day at LeBoeuf was memorable. The LeBoeuf fellows at the printer on the fateful D and S deal were Partner Charles Burger ("Chuck") and Associate Bill Rosenblatt. Chuck had been on the Yale Law Journal, and Bill was no slouch himself, having graduated from and done well at Columbia Law. They welcomed me. The informal atmosphere at LeBoeuf was evident in the way Bill and Chuck interacted. They called each other Bill and Chuck, rather than Mr. So-and-so.

During the interview process at LeBoeuf Senior Partner Joe Strauss had kindly added his influence to champion my cause at the firm. Joe was brilliant, and had been first in his class first year at Columbia Law. He was edgy, a bit prickly, and didn't suffer fools well. Joe had apparently been in a running feud with the non-legal but important office manager, Emily Essex, and neglected to tell Emily that I was arriving. When I darkened the doorstep, Emily seemed to take great pleasure in the fact that no office had been reserved for me, because Joe hadn't consulted her. She proceeded to make some highly visible efforts to find an office for me, demonstrating the importance of her job in keeping and maintaining order. Eventually I was situated in an office with a more senior lawyer Rich Baxter. Rich was a good guy who practiced in the Byzantine (to me) area of corporate tax law.

I was quite the curiosity as a lateral from Cravath. I tried to be a good boy, but would inevitably stumble. I asked innocently once whether I might get a supply of "routing slips," the little pink pieces of paper we used at Cravath that contained "To/From" language and room for a note. We would clip those slips on documents we were sending around the office. Nobody at LeBoeuf knew what routing slips were. Lawyers would just scribble the name of the intended recipient on the upper right-hand corner of the document, and let fly in the outbox. I was inwardly horrified at such a violation of the sanctity of a document. I got over it quickly.

Another treasured area of Cravath was the "Form Files." At the completion of each deal Cravath Associates would send documentation to the Form Files for use in other deals, often with extensive notations on particular negotiated matters, unusual provisions, whether the final documentation was favorable to one party or another, whether the precedent for the original draft favored one party or the other; things like that. Upon asking, I was told that LeBoeuf didn't have a Form Files. If you needed something, just ask around.

The most important difference in practice at LeBoeuf was the absence of a formal assignment system. At Cravath, an Associate was assigned to a particular Partner or team. If another Partner wanted to grab you, they had to ask or beg. At LeBoeuf, it was more of a free-for-all. I was subject to conflicting demands for my time, and things could get intense especially if the competing Partners themselves were not the best of friends.

I was generally left alone because people didn't want to mess with Joe too much. Early in my career at the firm I did most of my work for Joe, Chuck, and Bill. Chuck was hard-working, friendly, and cerebral. Bill had a very good and quick sense for the practical application of complex contractual provisions (and also was a great source of firm gossip). Joe was a law-firm god, loyal, and one of the best negotiators, draftsmen, and legal thinkers I've ever seen in action.

His written reviews of Associates could be pretty direct, too. In one Associate evaluation, not mine thankfully, he wrote that "X doesn't dissemble well." I had to look up "dissemble" but it gave me a good laugh.

I worked hard at LeBoeuf, and the informality was to my liking. Partners could take Associates out to lunch then, as an expense of the firm. Around noon, Associates working for Joe or Chuck would find themselves in their vicinity, with a supposed need for an urgent conversation, but really just hoping to hear the magic words, "Let's go to lunch." Joe would take us to the Broad Street Club, where we would be greeted by the friendly hostess there, Joe would eat his healthful fruit salad, muttering that he wanted something better, and <u>we</u> would be sure to <u>eat</u> something better.

Joe thought I was tenacious negotiator. I was incapable of his aggressiveness and attacking style; I just wanted to get certain things in the papers, and wouldn't move off them, maybe out of fear of what might happen if the provisions weren't included.

In those days, we represented insurance companies investing in private placements (namely, offerings to a limited group of big investors and not to the public at large). They would lend money to companies on agreed terms, and we would draft and negotiate the papers and attend to the closing. The preliminary term sheets prepared by the businessmen were good summaries of the terms but never sufficiently detailed from a legal standpoint. The lawyers had to write the papers with much more specificity, complicated defined terms, formulas, and the like.

The borrowers might squawk, and they often had very competent lawyers who knew how to hold our feet to the fire. One of those lawyers was a Partner at Houston's Baker & Botts; I wish I could remember his name. He was good, and nasty. I lost five pounds during a protracted negotiation with him. The deal cratered as I recall. Usually it was the "golden rule" that carried the day. That rule states that "He who has the gold rules." That version of the golden rule does not appear in the "Sermon on the Mount."

Sometimes a deal would make sense to a lender as a business matter, but pulling it together from a legal standpoint was a nightmare. Our client the lender signed up for a deal in the mid-1970's with a company that leased a certain kind of storage structure to farmers all over the country. The business people thought that the numerous little leasing deals could be combined and secure one note that would be held by our client, the lender. It made general sense and was a precursor of what would later be known as "securitization."

The practical problems for the deal back then sadly were numerous. The deal was small, under $5 million. The drafting was really tricky, involving the invention of a hypothetical note per lease, giving it terms, and then adding everything up. A computer program was required for the payment terms, including prepayments on the master note by reason of expirations or terminations of the underlying leases, or damage to or destruction of the leased structures. We did the drafting but the structures were in eleven states, requiring legal analysis and opinions from law firms in all those states.

The deal took forever to close, our firm's fee was $90,000, a lot for a deal that size back then, and nobody was really happy with the result. I am told that the CFO of the company was fired after the deal. Basically, a good idea was spoiled by the multiplicity of governing state laws, and the fact that we were aggregating numerous separate deals.

There were all kinds of other financial deals we handled. For a season in the late 1970's I became somewhat expert in the field of aircraft financing. Our client was interested on those deals, and I was involved in some novel structures. One was an "open-ended mortgage" for aircraft. That was similar to a utility mortgage, in which the mortgage lien would automatically cover all important tangible assets acquired by the utility, and the utility would be permitted to borrow against a percentage of that "borrowing base." Eventually, our client had enough of investments in aircraft, and my specialty became irrelevant and died from disuse. The bound volumes of the deals still look nice on my shelf.

I came up for Partner at LeBoeuf in late 1978. Between the time I arrived and 1978 the firm had stretched out the run for Partnership to eight years. The issue became for me the following: was I to be advanced a class, namely to the class of 1971, or was I to be considered for Partnership in 1978? My clear recollection was the latter, and Joe took up my cause. I remember the night when the powers-that-be discussed my case. My little cigars were piling up in the ash tray of my office, and office itself took on the character of a Superfund Site. (I gave up smoking those little cigars in 1984.)

After a few hours, Joe came to inform me that I was in as Partner, effective January 1, 1979, after six years as an Associate. He had threatened to leave the firm if the firm didn't honor the promise to me. The way he put it was that if I asked him to leave, he would. It obviously didn't get to that point, but I'll never forget that whole scene and his loyalty.

On reflection, I don't fault Doug Hawes, the head of the Corporate Department. Doug had a lot on his mind beyond the particulars of one Associate. Since I left a good situation at Cravath, however, I knew precisely what my deal was: I would take the risk of my performance being inadequate at LeBoeuf, but I shouldn't have to take the risk of any firm decision to extend the run to Partnership, which was beyond my control.

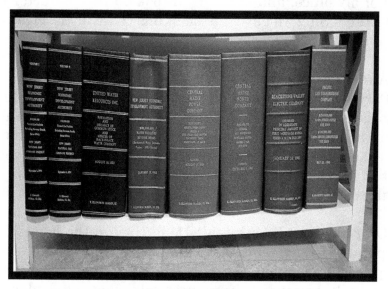

One of El's bookshelves of bound volumes
containing deal papers. This type of
literature does not usually show up
on any "best-seller" lists.

32

Cabbages and Kings, Semicolons and Wings

In a broad sense, my career as a lawyer can be broken down almost by decade. In the 1970's I was learning how to be a lawyer. In the 1980's I was learning how to be a Partner. In the 1990's I was learning how to be a senior Partner, who would have the crazy idea to leave the law and undertake the highly under-remunerated occupation of touring folk guitarist.

As I mentioned before I didn't really have a close, personal relationship with the triune God until much later in my life. I did know God had intervened in certain situations, as recounted, and I had experienced "signals of transcendence," although that wonderful term wasn't in my lexicon until I was nearly 70.

In this setting, the temptation is for me to breeze through the next twenty years of my legal career and go from LeBoeuf to the meat, shall we say. I must resist that. I need to share some unusual legal issues and situations I had to confront. The word "wings" in the Chapter title is a tortured reference to the aforesaid aircraft deals -- tortured because a number of those deals involved helicopters, and they have "rotor blades" not wings. We'll get to the fascinating issue of the semicolon in a little while.

My friend, mentor, and firm rabbi Joe Strauss died tragically of cancer in 1984. He was in physical decline before that. Seeing Joe like that was unbearable for me. I really couldn't handle it. I honor my Partner John Dinn, who was there for Joe during all of that. I wasn't, or at least I wasn't as much as I should have been. I remember the day when the firm moved Joe's desk and possessions out of his corner office. He insisted on being brought from his home in a wheelchair to be there and make a statement. It was an awful scene. He looked into my eyes, and I just saw pain, anger, and darkness. Five years later firm Chairman Don Greene, to my great surprise, gave me Joe's old office.

One of my children was old enough to know Joe before his decline. One day son Jon came to the office with me. Joe looked at his mop of blond hair, and said, with affection, "Hey, kid, where'd ya get that hair?"

My practice was changing by 180 degrees. Instead of representing insurance company lenders to companies, I became outside counsel for companies who wanted to issue securities and borrow money. My clients went from Teachers Insurance and Annuity Association and CIGNA eventually to Central Maine Power Company (the largest electric utility in Maine), Maine Yankee Atomic Power Co., United Water Resources Inc., New Jersey Resources, The Columbia Gas System, and Orange and Rockland Utilities.

Having spent my early years representing those with the money, I went over to the side of those wanting the money, or at least wanting to borrow it. As lender's counsel, I had been tasked with the responsibility of making sure a borrower couldn't find some loophole to wriggle through and adversely hurt the interests of the lender. As borrower's counsel, I understood the interests of the lender, but I needed to make sure that the contractual restrictions on my client didn't pinch too tight and have unforeseen and adverse consequences. My fear was always that a seemingly harmless provision could somehow trip the client up in some unrelated area.

For example, let's say that the papers prohibited subsidiaries of the borrower from incurring debt. That made some sense from a lender's viewpoint, but what was "debt?" Also, what about routine transactions, or transactions in which a subsidiary of a company would borrow from the company, its parent? Or what about a subsidiary borrowing from another subsidiary? Borrower's counsel had to be very vigilant in the area of these types of restrictions.

I did billions of dollars worth of financings in my career. When I see the astronomical amounts involved in deals today, however, I think that one huge tech deal would dwarf in dollars all my deals combined. Still, a few billion dollars or so in a career isn't pocket change even in this world.

It was hard enough to draft and close deals. Sometimes the word-processing equipment threw you scary curves. A friend of mine at Cravath told me the story of a terrible thing that happened to a lawyer once in the early days of word-processing. There had been an intense negotiation of a financial term in one of his deals, and the papers were redrafted with the agreed-upon number in it. The secretary who typed the re-draft failed to "save" the change, however. As a result, when the execution copies were produced, the text had reverted to the previous number. As my nice friends from Salt Lake City might say, "Oh, my heck!"

171

Worse words than those were said in that situation, and loudly, amidst mistrust that took a long time to heal.

That story stuck with me throughout my practice. I was more comfortable with linotype at the printer, where you knew when whole lines of type had been changed through physical means. You would proofread the whole lines and "slug" the rest to make sure no lines had been dropped. I know that is from the stone age, and that electronic word-processing is much better, but I simply felt that I had no control of where the gremlins might emerge.

Here's a case in point: I had a nice vacation with my wife and some of our kids at the Greenbrier in West Virginia, my favorite resort of all time. There were three problems: Jimmy got sick on something, it was winter, and I was negotiating a bank loan for a client. It was a $1.3 Billion revolving-credit agreement. The concierge was bringing up faxes for me to review, and I was sending them out. The papers were finalized, and a couple of weeks later I went with signed signature pages to the closing at the offices of the bank's law firm.

The Associates there looked a little puzzled that a Partner would show up at a paper-pushing party. I told them that $1.3 Billion had my attention. I started going through the pages of the agreement, kind of eyeballing things. A few pages into the document, right in a sensitive area covering financial restrictions on our client, the pages didn't line up. In other words, the last word of one page didn't flow into the correct first word of the next page. The youngsters on the other side were mortified. What had happened was that some of the pages had come from one printing machine at the firm, and the others from another.

The twain had not met. They fixed the document, and I took a copy and left.

Here's what would have happened if I had missed that problem: the document would have been put away, and forgotten, until the outside accountant months later would be called upon to confirm that our client was in compliance with the financial restrictions. The accountants would find the glitch, there would be an uproar, and inside General Counsel of the company would rightly call me and ask, *"What in the heck happened?"* He might not be so polite.

These anecdotes illustrate just a couple of the ways in which things can go wrong in even the most sophisticated of transactions. Sometimes there are actual matters of legal substance. I was drafting a document to protect a corporate client against unwanted takeovers. The draft included provisions for super-majority voting rights in certain situations – meaning, that certain transactions could take place only with the affirmative vote of 80% of the shares of the company.

I looked at comparable papers used in the case of another company in that state. When I looked at state law, however, I discovered that the law itself dictated the vote required for certain transactions, and it was 51%. The anti-takeover provisions for the other company didn't take account of the state law. I decided that in the cases where state law provided the voting requirement, I would have our document state that it controls unless our provisions violated state law. I did it that way to cover our client in the immediate situation, but also to cover the case if the state law were amended in the future to change the voting requirement from 51% or to eliminate that voting provision entirely.

We wrote it that way, and nobody thought about the issue until a few years later, when a corporate raider went after the other company. The company interposed its anti-takeover document as a defense, the attacker alleged that the provisions violated state law, the matter went to court, and the court agreed with the attacker and struck down the anti-takeover defense. The Board of our client asked whether our firm had gotten it right. It was such a joy to us that the inside corporate counsel was able to review our papers and report that we had.

One of my favorite stories involves the semicolon, mentioned in the title of this Chapter. I can honestly report that millions of dollars turned on that semicolon, and that's why I spent so much time and painstaking effort in drafting legal documents.

The client utility company wanted to buy in some of the bonds that it had issued years earlier under an ancient mortgage indenture, written in 1929. The interest rates were in the teens then, and these old bonds were paying 3 and 4%. The company could probably buy them at 40 cents on the dollar. You might ask why would they even want to do that. Why would they borrow money at a higher rate to buy and retire those cheaper bonds? The reason was that this company was running low on "borrowing base." It was financing the building of a plant, but couldn't borrow against the plant until the plant was in operation. (I think I'm getting this part right, as context.) If they could buy in the bonds, they would get 100 cents on the dollar as borrowing base, and it would cost them only 40 cents on the dollar. Put another way, if the company retired an outstanding bond it could issue another bond for an equal principal amount, even if the company paid less to buy the old bond in.

There was a problem under the old indenture, however. There was a semicolon in the relevant provision that indicated that the company couldn't <u>buy</u> the bonds but had to <u>redeem</u> them at the redemption price, which was 102 cents on the dollar.

One very able Partner of our firm wanted to read the semicolon as a comma; I believed that we couldn't do that. I think he knew, too, but wanted to make the case anyway. We consulted a third lawyer, a bright guy and friend of both of ours. The friend said that, regrettably, it really <u>was</u> a semicolon and not a comma with an ancient fly-speck over it. The company had to redeem the bonds. They did the redemption and the difference as I recall was in the range of 12-15 million dollars. On reflection, I think I understand the policy behind the restriction and, in any event, no one can blame us for drafting it since none of us was alive then!

The hardest type of contract I ever had to deal with was this sort of mortgage indenture for a public utility, like a gas or an electric company. A New York corporate lawyer could go through a whole career and never have to write or review one of those. I had to work on <u>two</u> of them, from <u>scratch</u>. The first was one I reviewed from the lender's perspective; the second I prepared as company counsel. The process in each case was torturous.

I'm looking right now at my marked-up copy of the excellent first draft by the distinguished Boston lawyer

Andrew M. Wood, Esq., of the law firm Gaston Snow & Ely Bartlett. It dates from 1980. I kept it to remind myself of the pain. The document is entitled the "First Mortgage Indenture and Deed of Trust" for an electric company that we can call B.

God only knows how long it took Andy to write that monster. The printed (not typed) text is 168 single-spaced pages. The marked draft containing <u>my</u> comments with proposed language totals 251 pages. The definitions alone in the document run for 22 single-spaced pages. (In the document as signed, the definitions occupy 30 printed pages.)

If you wanted to read this document for, say, fun, you might want to enjoy the definition of "Permitted Liens." It runs for four single-spaced pages. Or perhaps you would like to learn about an "Additional Property Certificate," the definition of which also runs for four pages. What characters! What a plot must be unfolding!

It took me two full eight-hour working days to review and comment on just the <u>definitions</u>. It took me two <u>weeks</u> of agonizing review to produce my draft with comments. To honor the effort of the draftsman of this great document, I provided draft language for Andy's consideration. I didn't just scribble "fix" this or that. I had to figure out <u>how</u> to fix it, and offer language. Our first meeting on the document took three full days, as Andy properly and carefully considered every word of every comment.

At the time I worked on this, I had just recently been named a Partner. <u>Nobody</u> at our law firm had <u>ever</u> written a utility mortgage or, to my knowledge, reviewed and commented on one in its entirety. The B deal closed in January of 1981, with the issuance of $30 million of "First Mortgage Bonds, Series A 14.25% due 1995." I'm not sure whether the company ever issued any more Bonds under that indenture. I heard rumblings later that they thought the terms were too restrictive. My clients and I were probably the reason (my word) or the blame (their word, no doubt) for that.

Years later, near the end of my career as a lawyer, I had to <u>write</u> one of these bad boys for Central Maine Power Company. It was to be a second mortgage, called a General and Refunding Mortgage. I can't seem to find my draft. Maybe I didn't want to be reminded of <u>that</u> degree of pain.

It took me months to produce a draft. It received a careful review and comment from another eminent Boston attorney, Frank Porter, Esq., of Choate Hall & Stewart. It never got signed. Central Maine was bought by another company, which had other ideas about financing and didn't need the mortgage.

Was I disappointed? My heavens, no. I had to cobble the document together from a bunch of other models. Despite all the work I did, I had the nagging fear that something might not "work" in the administration of the document, with all the fine-pencil work needed from the company's operational and financial people. Moreover, the approach in the document was different from what they were used to in the mortgage that was being replaced. That having been said, if the company ever wants to do one of those mortgages, it should definitely start with my draft, and give it a fresh look.

You can see by now the toll that this kind of work might take on a person, especially someone with a wife and four kids, commuting back and forth between the Apple and Mountain Lakes, wanting to play guitar more, and feeling a bit burned out. I had 28 years to give the law in NYC, it turns out. I took early retirement in 2000, at age 52.

I would love to list the names of all the wonderful colleagues and friends I had at LeBoeuf, but I would leave someone out, and that would grieve both of us. Nevertheless, I must thank the loyal secretaries I had over the years, Marianne Brown Berke, Justine Zaleski, and John Lamanna, who always rose to the occasion when I was under pressure, and were wonderful representatives of the firm to our clients.

A concluding note on the firm. In the early 1990's the firm produced a video called "The LeBoeuf Story." Our firm Chairman Don Greene narrated it, and many of my colleagues and friends can be seen in it talking about the firm and its clients. The purpose was not to get clients so much as to build esprit de corps among the various offices that the firm had opened when it was in expansion mode.

Some people mocked it, but I loved it. Maybe I'm biased, because as the credits run I am shown playing guitar in one of the firm conference rooms. I'm looking pretty good for me: suit, suspenders, more hair, less gray, and doing a decent job on "The Blarney Pilgrim Jig."

A firm wag once said, "Well, it's not exactly 'Gone with the Wind.'" Sadly, it was. Twelve years after I left the firm, it declared bankruptcy in the largest law firm failure in American history. Sic Transit Gloria. RIP LeBoeuf.

33

Music in the 1980's: El as Troubadour

I didn't have a lot of time to listen to music in the late 1970's and early 1980's. I actually did like Disco, loved the movie "Saturday Night Fever" from the late 1970's, and still crave a white suit like Tony's. "Staying alive, staying alive!" still pierces my brain, and I can't to this day figure out how the Bee Gees sang so high.

Things eventually picked up for me. I had two areas of musical interest. One was singing and songwriting. The other was guitar instrumentals. The songwriting came first, and I'll touch on it first. It eventually faded in favor of instrumental guitar music.

As our four children were growing up, I had the urge to write songs about them. I had done some songwriting before, but I hadn't publicized it much or really pushed myself to raise my game. Upon the tragic death of Phil Ochs in April 1976, I wrote a song about him and sent a cassette to his sister Sonny, who at the time lived in Far Rockaway. I got a nice note from her containing the sad but true statement: "If only Phil had known how much people cared."

I wrote some other songs, and found a great venue for trying them out, the Folk City club in Greenwich Village on West 3d Street. Thereupon commenced a rather strange

179

little season of my life. On Mondays I would bring my guitar to the firm, and work at the firm in a suit until 5 PM. Then I would change into more informal clothes, grab the guitar and some dinner in the Village, and then go over to Folk City and wait my turn to sing a couple songs during "Open Mic Night." I might not get on stage until 10 or 11, and wouldn't get home until the wee hours. I might even accompany some friends to play at another open mic place afterwards. It symbolized the clash of cultures between music and law that would intensify for me in the 1990's and lead to my decision to take early retirement from the firm in 2000.

The first night I did Folk City, I heard someone call out "Sonny" to the lady who ran Open Mic Night. It was none other than Sonny Ochs, Phil Ochs's sister! Tell me that wasn't a God-at-work moment! Sonny remembered my song and cassette from ten years earlier, and treated me very well during the nights I played there. She gave me good advice, too. After I sang a somewhat brooding, introspective song, she suggested favoring a more upbeat message.

One time my sister came down to hear me sing. I didn't get on stage until midnight, and the crowd was pretty small, but Franny was there cheering me on. I asked Sonny if she would record it, and she did. It was a song I wrote called "Giants in the Land." It turned out to be a Finalist in the Folk category of a songwriting contest I later entered called the "4th Annual Mid-Atlantic Song Contest." It was really a national contest, and some talented folks from Nashville won big that year. Of the three songs I wrote for my kids and entered, one song was named a Semi-Finalist and two were Honorable Mention.

I collected my thoughts on songwriting, wrote them down, and conducted a few workshops on the subject. I have since lost those notes, sadly. I have recordings of myself singing those three songs for the kids. Maybe I'll enter them in another contest and see how they do thirty years later!

As mentioned above, songwriting kind of faded as my desire to do guitar music greatly intensified. There were a few reasons for that. First was my suspicion that as hard as I might work to write songs, Mary Chapin Carpenter's worst song (if there were such a thing) would be better than my best one. Secondly, songwriters I like are masters of indirection, a perfect example being Mary's song "Stones in the Road." My training as a corporate lawyer, however, favored just the opposite: precision, specificity, and clarity. Dylan's compelling image of the "answer blowing in the wind" might in my hands end up as a geography lesson with coordinates and the precise location of the "answer." Hahaha. Finally, I was finding people in the world -- really knowledgeable people and great guitarists -- who were interested in my instrumental music. What a kick that was!

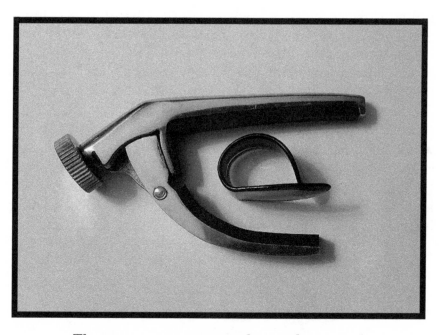

The capo seems prepared to make a meal
out of the thumb pick.

34

Music in the 1980's:
El as Guitar-Picker

An enthusiastic audience is the best encouragement to a musician. Money might well trump that, but big dollars usually aren't a "problem" (Hahaha) in the world of fingerstyle guitar. We can be pretty big fish in some pretty small ponds.

A few years ago, Art Edelstein, a very knowledgeable author and music scholar, wrote a review of a recording of mine and called me "the king of CGDGAD tuning." I greatly appreciated the compliment but told someone later that if I were royalty, my domain was quite small and I had no subjects. That having been said and modesty having no place in the music biz (and triple gerunds being rare and wonderful), I still beat it like a drum.

I have to back up some – say 25 years. I am getting <u>way</u> too far ahead of myself.

In 1980 I was on a guitar-picking plateau, or treading water, or the subject of some other negative metaphor. Things had to improve a lot before I could be an aquatic life-form of any type in the pond of fingerpicking guitar.

The decade of the 1980's, moreover, involved the birth of three of our children, the childhood experiences of all four, hours of commuting to and from NYC, and on the law-firm front, large corporate deals, important client relationships involving many trips to Maine and other places, and my work heading up the Summer Associate program at the firm. That long and clunky sentence does not contain the word "guitar."

During all that, a miracle happened. Through nothing short of an Act of God, I went from a mildly accomplished dilettante on guitar to someone with the potential to draw people all over the world into my musical world.

That decade positioned me to record and release fourteen recordings, four DVD's (and be included on others), and numerous books of tab/music for Mel Bay Publications and my own Piney Ridge Music. I will share below some factors in that substantial increase in "my game," but don't think for a moment that the way these things came together was anything short of miraculous. (If nothing else, let's not forget I am a guy with cerebral palsy.)

The first factor I mention is so ordinary that I almost forgot it. It involved, of all things, the guitar itself. I was playing my Martin D-21 with medium strings, and the action had come up over the years. I didn't know about action. I didn't know about using light rather than medium-gauge strings. I didn't realize that the neck geometry on that guitar wasn't right for me. I really "didn't know nuttin'" about the instrument I was trying to play.

I finally sold the Martin, bought another Martin, sold it and went through guitars in the way that the proverbial drunken sailor goes through bottles of beer. I kept wondering why I couldn't play smoothly John Renbourn's arrangement of the "English Dance" when I was playing on big guitars with high action and medium strings. Hello! Wake up, El. It took me most of that decade to learn a little something about the instrument, and gradually playing got easier.

I liked Martins, owned some Goodalls and Tippins, but came to favor Franklin guitars, made by luthier wizard Nick Kukich. Stefan Grossman, whom I will discuss later, put me on to Nick and his guitars. Since then, Franklin has created the "El McMeen Signature Model" OM-size guitar.

I remember that on a Labor Day late in the decade of the 1980's Renbourn's arrangement of "Mist-Covered Mountains of Home" finally came under my fingers. I was so afraid I would lose it that I took the guitar to a neighbor's party we attended and played it over and over under a tree. Now I do that tune in CGDGAD tuning, with different chords and favoring the thumb rather than the fingers. Nevertheless, achieving some degree of proficiency in John's "ripple" technique was a breakthrough for me. I'll get to technique next. What I want to emphasize now is that I starting finding out that the guitar itself could and should actually do some of the work!

As to technique, I mentioned earlier in this book that I strummed guitar and played almost exclusively alternating-bass, using the thumb and the middle finger. I suspected that I needed better chops. I bought a Homespun Tapes lesson called "Beginning Fingerpicking Guitar," presented by Doc and Merle Watson. I remember that it had "Spike Driver's Blues" on it.

We were in Maine for vacation in the summer of 1985, and I really dug into that tape series. I couldn't get very far because playing with the thumb and one finger didn't cut it. Maybe the late, great Merle Travis (not to be confused with Merle Watson) could play that way, but Travis wasn't playing fast notes on successive treble strings, nor triplets on one string. (The latter technique was not on the beginners' series.) I had to learn to play with at least two fingers and a thumb, and it took a while.

A sad thing happened shortly after that Maine trip. I had been listening over-and-over to Merle Watson talking on that tape, and then two months later he was gone. He died tragically at age 36 in a tractor accident near his home in North Carolina. That hit me hard because in a sense he and I had been visiting together for hours, and he was trying to help me be a better guitarist. I went into mourning for Merle's family.

Shortly after that I saw a little box ad in Frets Magazine for cassette lessons produced by something called "Stefan Grossman's Guitar Workshop." The ad really intrigued me, so I shot $50 off to the P.O. Box mentioned in the ad. A few days later my secretary tells me, "Somebody named Stefan Grossman is on the phone." Stefan happened to be in town from Rome, where he lived. He called to find out what kind of music I was interested in – blues, ragtime, classic rag, or folk rag. I was honored that he would take the time to call me, but was clueless about the different genres. He recommended the "Advanced Fingerpicking Guitar" series of tapes, which turned out to be both enjoyable and challenging. I was amazed at how effortlessly Stefan played that difficult music.

I will discuss Stefan in more detail later. I ended up buying in that period over $700 worth of those tape lessons. If anyone were to inquire about my "formal training," I would point to all the techniques and different genres of music I explored in those wonderful cassettes. (The media in Stefan's workshop are now primarily DVD's, downloads, and books.)

I drove myself to learn the material on the tapes. After a few years, I said to myself, "El, maybe you don't <u>have</u> to learn <u>every</u> single tune; concentrate on the ones you like." I was so driven that I hadn't even thought of skipping something. I ended up donating all the tapes and accompanying materials to Northfield Mt. Hermon School in the 1990's.

Based on Stefan's materials, I started to explore different guitar tunings. For 20 years I had stuck to standard guitar tuning, EADGBE, with the exception of my excursion into Geoff Muldaur's tune "Mole's Moan," in Open G tuning, DGDGBD. It was probably helpful to me that I wasn't really well-versed in standard tuning. My empty mind would serve as an "open" mind to "open" tunings.

During this productive period, I was listening to a cassette I bought from Stefan's workshop, with the name "Irish Reels, Jigs, Hornpipes, and Airs," featuring really talented guitarists playing something called "traditional Irish music." I had heard only a few examples of that type of music before, and never as guitar solos. It was a great recording.

The playing of one of the British guitarists on there really resonated with me. His name was Dave Evans and his music just shimmered. I consulted the accompanying book, and he was playing in a very unusual tuning, "CGDGAD." The result was this glorious sound. I had to learn it, so I explored all of his arrangements in that folio. They rocked my world.

As I became more accomplished on guitar in that period, I would keep one guitar in standard tuning and the other in CGDGAD. Eventually, I tuned both guitars to CGDGAD and played almost exclusively in that tuning, with an occasional foray into DADGAD. Much later I would write books with my arrangements in a more conventional tuning, Dropped D tuning (DADGBE), so that guitarists could explore my arrangements without radically re-tuning their guitars. Dropped D could capture 90% of the musical atmosphere, but not 100%.

I reached out for Dave via e-mail as I was getting more familiar with the tuning. He explained how he found it. He was experimenting with tunings in the 1960's and was aware of DADGAD and Open G minor tuning, DGDGBbD. He preferred Open D, DADF#AD, and Open G, DGDGBD. Going back to G minor tuning, he found a solution to a problem he was having by lowering the bottom string to C, producing CGDGBbD. Eventually, he said, the CGDGAD tuning in an almost mystical way "found him," and he lowered the pitch of the second string to A from Bb.

The tuning, or something very close to it, may well have been an ancient, rarely used, Hawaiian tuning. As far as I'm concerned, however, Dave Evans put it on the map. He gets full credit. Better yet, he gets extra credit. Dave, you are The Man.

I believe the Lord loaned or gifted that tuning to me to popularize and make it accessible to guitarists at every level, beginner, intermediate, and advanced. The reason I believe this was a supernatural God-at-work moment is that if I hadn't picked up that cassette with the long name, I never would have found the tuning. If I hadn't found that tuning, I simply would have had no influence in fingerstyle guitar music. That tuning is what inspired me to arrange music, nearly 200 tunes in CGDGAD alone, from the "American Patrol" march to Bach's "Jesu, Joy of Man's Desiring." If I have any legacy in music at all, it's popularizing the CGDGAD tuning.

What I've been doing in this Chapter is attempting to piece together what was happening to me in the 1980's in the area of fingerstyle guitar. So far, we have dealt with the guitar as an instrument; techniques; exposure to different genres of music; and the wonderful CGDGAD tuning. We now must probe the world of Celtic music. Come with me on a journey on a train, the daily world of the commuter from NJ to NYC.

As mentioned, I was into Stefan's taped guitar lessons big-time. On my train rides between NJ and NYC I would listen to the cassettes on a portable cassette-player, while reviewing and notating the accompanying tab/music. On a train full of commuters, I've got headphones on and am poring over guitar music.

One day a gentleman sits down next to me. His name is Caleb Crowell. It turns out he is a fellow Harvard guy (ten or so years senior to me, and with a better record at Harvard, I might add). He is in the world of publishing and, of all things, an expert in and lover of Celtic music. He also is a guitarist. He sees me, this guy absorbed in music. We get talking. The particular tune I'm learning is a Celtic tune.

The next day we meet on the train, and Caleb hands me a cassette he made the night before. It contains multiple renditions of the tune I was working on, either sung or played on all kinds of different instruments, like pipes, harp, and even whistle. As I start to spread my own tiny, immature wings and fly in the area of arranging Celtic tunes, he would do this over and over again, enriching my ears and mind on how to perform those tunes. Caleb's contributions during that season were invaluable to my knowledge and growth as a guitarist and artist.

In particular, piano and harp treatments of the tunes I was learning revealed to me the technique of arpeggiation. I was moving away from the boom-chick sound of alternating bass into a world of presenting melody notes in the course of eighth-note arpeggios from the bass strings to the treble strings. If this guitar stuff is Greek to you, just think of the way a harp is often played, not the bursts of notes, but flowing, atmospheric music.

What are the chances that all of this would result from an encounter on a commuter train? Tell me all that was coincidental, especially when it happened precisely at the time in my life when I needed it!

As mentioned, Caleb also provided sung versions of Irish melodies. That music led me to understand matters of phrasing, harkening back to my A Cappella Choir experience at Mt. Hermon. The phrasing involved dynamics, meaning loudness and softness, and matters of speed and rhythmic flexibility ("rubato"). Over many years my playing would begin to emulate the human voice even more perhaps than the harp. One more technique, however, was required to draw nearer to accomplishing this, the "slow-hand vibrato."

Doing guitar renditions of sung music presents difficulties of arrangement and technique. Sung music often revels in repetition, whereas repetition can devolve into repetitiveness in an instrumental version. In working up an arrangement of a sung tune, we need to avoid the extremes of, on the one hand, boring repetitiveness and on the other, attempts to vary the tune that are quirky or jarring.

On the technical side, a guitarist must find a way to sustain notes, since many beautiful melodies require notes to be held and savored. Think "Amazing Grace" and "Danny Boy." The usual technique on a classical/nylon-string guitar involves moving the fretted string side-to-side, parallel with the fingerboard. That technique does not always work well on a steel-string guitar. It is often more effective to work the string up-and-down, perpendicular to the neck of the guitar, slowly, using the fretting arm rather than just the fretting finger and thumb behind the neck. Think Eric Clapton.

Stefan Grossman taught me that technique, and I have shared it with others. Stefan has great left-hand control, and has employed the technique in all genres of music, from Celtic to country blues.

As I was processing and applying all this tremendous information, my interest was further piqued by a lovely, perhaps seminal, recording by guitarist Martin Simpson in

1989. It was on the Shanachie label and called "Leaves of Life." The album contained guitar instrumentals of beautiful Celtic songs, that is, sung pieces. To this day, 30 years later, that album stands out for its beauty and the creative ways that the melodies are presented.

Late in the decade I did a little home-recording of my own arrangements of tunes, and sent it to Stefan, who in the interim had moved back to the States. I was delighted when he asked me to do some cassette instructional series on my own arrangements of Celtic, spiritual, and Christmas music. It was especially gratifying to think that only a few years earlier it was I who was learning from cassettes in his workshop.

Stefan has become a dear friend, and through his support and guidance, I was able to have two of my recordings released by the prestigious Shanachie label. He also introduced me to Mr. William Bay, head of Mel Bay Publications, for whom I have written several books. Stefan, in addition, produced three of my instructional DVD's for his workshop, along with the performance DVD called "The Guitar Artistry of El McMeen."

There were supernatural elements at work in my association with Stefan. We had been trying to get together for lunch, but something would always come up. A few days after lunch plans had gone awry, I flew to Boston for a closing on a financing for Central Maine Power Company. The night before big closings I never went out to any concerts or anything like that in Boston, preferring to keep my nose to the grindstone. This time, however, I happened to see a local paper lying around, picked it up, and saw, of all things, a notice that Stefan and John Renbourn were playing that very night at a club in Cambridge, across the river. Having made sure that our deal was in good order, I took a cab to the show, and had the great pleasure of hanging out with Stefan and John at intermission and after the show. You may think I'm overdoing it, but tell me that was just a coincidence.

One last note in this recitation. I did find some outlets to perform music in public. I couldn't do much of it, in light of family and law-firm responsibilities, but I got to do some. I opened for a folksinger in the mid-1980's in the fine "Minstrel Show" coffeehouse concert series under the auspices of the Folk Project in NJ. The main act paid me the ultimate compliment of saying I was never to open for him again. That's a good thing in the folk world. In addition, I played in church, and I even had a gig on Saturday nights at a local restaurant in Mountain Lakes called Phoebe Snow. I still have somewhere a copy of the little ad for that gig in the local newspaper. Those were to be seeds that would sprout into my touring during 1999-2002 with guitarist Larry Pattis throughout the US.

Sign in "God's country, Huntingdon County region."

35

More God-at-Work: Jim Ensor

As I finish writing the last Chapter, I still find incredible all the things that happened during the decade of the 1980's. I haven't even dipped into family anecdotes, relationships with friends, and like personal matters that are important in anyone's life. I will mention, as I sit here typing, that I got my revenge on our cat Millie: for a change, I actually awoke her in the middle of the night. I wanted to finish writing the last Chapter and start this one. She's back asleep on the bed here in the study, with front paws in the air.

I'm not going to detail my recordings and books in the 1990's and thereafter, nor reminisce about concerts I did alone or with Larry Pattis. Relevant info is out there, including articles that kind people have written about me in various magazines. I need to shift the focus to more eternal matters, spiritual things. Musical, vocational, and family matters will most definitely come into play in that context.

I must start with the strange case of my relationship with a pastor named Jim Ensor. I have just recounted many things that were happening in my life in the 1980's, and before. Jim's life was quite different. He pastored the "First Church of God" in Rocky Ford, Colorado. To find Rocky Ford, you go South from Denver, hit Pueblo, turn left, and go for miles until you find fields of watermelons. At least that's my recollection. How in the world would a lawyer/musician in the Big Apple meet up and become close friends with a pastor in Rocky Ford, the self-declared "Sweet Melon Capital of the World?"

It happened this way: In the mid-1980's I made a home recording on cassette of my performances of some spiritual and gospel tunes. I did it on my trusty Advent cassette-recorder, with no editing and only the reverb that comes from recording in an empty room in our house. The playing was OK, but the sound was a little rough. In addition, I recorded the same song on it more than once in an attempt to give the recording an atmosphere of a recurring theme. I advertised the tape in Frets Magazine.

I received a letter with a lot of questions from a pastor named Jim Ensor from the aforesaid Rocky Ford. I really didn't have the time or inclination to go point-by-point. I just shipped a cassette off to Pastor Ensor saying that I hoped it was OK, and if not, not to tell me about it. I was being funny, not a jerk.

A few days later, I received a cassette from <u>him</u>, containing a recording of some music from his church. It was kind of throw-back Southern gospel, yet sincere. I thanked him for it, and figured that was that. Then I received <u>another</u> tape from him, this time containing some flatpicking by a man named Dan Crary and one named Tony Rice. Those guys were monster flatpickers, and I told him so. I sent <u>him</u> some Celtic guitar stuff on cassette. Then he sent <u>me</u> some Jerry Douglas, Mr. Dobro. He was educating me on bluegrass!

One time I was on the train listening to one of his tapes, kind of zoning out, when he started talking to me on the tape! I about jumped out of my seat. Imagine this yourself. You have headphones on listening to music, and then a voice comes on, totally unexpectedly. That was the scene.

What ensued was a relationship built on the exchange of cassette tapes. Sometimes I would receive three or four tapes from him in a week. It was about music, to be sure, but more importantly and subliminally it was about the Christian faith, his church, the music at his church, and even the subject-matter of his upcoming sermons.

This went on for years, until one day he invited me out to Rocky Ford to play guitar at the church's yearly "God and Country" service. I flew out and met Jim, his family, and a bunch of his church friends. I was a fish out of water in that atmosphere, with a sincere man of God in a little church out in the heat of southern Colorado. But I had a great time.

One day at a pizza shop in town he asked me whether I was a Christian. I said I <u>thought</u> so, which no doubt indicated to him that I really <u>wasn't</u>. (If you have to <u>think</u> about it, you're <u>not</u>.) I recounted the usual facts you trot out when you really don't know Jesus: church attendance and trying to be a good boy. (I didn't mention the "Offering Plate Caper" of my youth, discussed in Chapter 4.) He didn't press the point.

Why do I mention all this? Nobody short of Jesus can pray you into the Kingdom of God, but if anyone could, it would be Jim Ensor. I can't know until Glory, but I have the strong sense that the things of a spiritual nature I will recount in this book somehow resulted in the heavenlies from the prayers for me by Jim Ensor back in the 1980's and 1990's.

Jim had heart problems, and later had a stroke. I took son Dan out to visit Jim and his lovely wife Rozan before he passed away in 2001. After Jim died, Rozan and I began to exchange tapes. It seemed only natural. She died in 2009 after a heroic battle with cancer – and after receiving her college degree, with Honors, at age 58. She was one warm, fine lady.

I took a cassette recorder with me on the last trip to see Jim. Dan and I recorded a running travelogue into the machine, and it is part of the McMeen family lore. It also befits Jim, and my relationship with that wonderful man. He would have liked that. I'm getting emotional now, at 4 AM, as I write this.

36

Sparta (NJ, Not the Greek One)

The musical seeds of the 1980's turned into fruit in the 1990's and thereafter. That fruit included studio recordings of guitar instrumentals, video guitar lessons for Stefan, books, two summers of teaching at the Swannanoa Gathering near Asheville, NC, and preparation for the big decision to leave the practice of law and pursue guitar-playing more seriously. The latter decision was triggered in 1998 by my second summer of teaching at Swannanoa. I asked my good friend and fellow teacher there Scott Ainslie whether he thought I really could have some impact as a touring guitarist. He wrote me a thoughtful, encouraging, and informative letter on the subject, with the cautionary note that one doesn't usually get rich playing folk guitar.

In September 1998 I went in to see our firm Chairman Sam Sugden and told him that I wanted to wind down my practice of law, and do something crazy like go play guitar. I would help in easing other Partners into representation of my clients. That process was not so easy, since some clients actually seemed to like me, or at least were used to me and my ways. They weren't so keen on some Attorney X coming on board.

It all worked out, however, and after a short stint as "Of Counsel" at the firm, I was gone. Accompanying me was my little metal nameplate from the wall next the door of my corner office. (I still have the nameplates from my various offices at Cravath and LeBoeuf.)

On the home front, things were percolating as well. Jon had gone off to college at Lafayette, graduated, ran a local landscaping business, and was looking into law school. The other kids were either in or looking at college. Boy, I had to be sure I counted the pennies right on this wild idea of taking early retirement from a big law firm to do guitar gigs.

Sheila and I had been in Mountain Lakes for nearly 28 years, and in 2002 were thinking we needed a change of scenery. The kids had all gone through the public-school system in Mountain Lakes. Moreover, having lived in an old Laker house for so long, we were wondering what it might be like to go to a newer house, hopefully with the master bedroom on the first floor.

It came to a head in Fall 2002. We decided to look at houses in different towns. We liked a house in Lambertville, NJ, near the border with PA, and were one phone call away from doing a deal there. In the interim, however, I ran across some listings for Sparta, about 20 miles away from Mountain Lakes. We went to look at a house there, but I had misread the listing notice and the house did not have the MBR on the first floor. However, we were intrigued by Sparta. A "little bird" or "still, small voice" seemed to be telling me to do Sparta.

We contracted for a house in Sparta, closed in mid-December, and moved on December 30, 2002, after a storm had generously contributed a couple feet of snow to our new property.

Some of our kids were stunned by the speed with which they were uprooted. Jimmy reminds me that we told him by voicemail while he was at Harvard. That was bad. We later sought and received forgiveness. All of us did like the big, new house. The other house would sell five months later.

The Sparta move presented a sweet irony for me. If we had been in ancient Sparta, I with my physical problems would have been placed on a rock outside of town to provide a tasty snack for the predator-animal crowd. As it was, it took me days to recover from packing up the old house and doing the move. Son Jon does a pretty good imitation of what I looked like during and after the move.

If you are wondering why I'm getting into this level of detail, the reason is this: I had the greatest spiritual awakening of my life in Sparta, NJ. I believe that I was "baptized in the Holy Spirit" in Sparta. Before I get to that, I need to address the matter of being "born again," which usually precedes being baptized in the Holy Spirit.

If you are reading this and are not a Christian, please continue reading. You will encounter some amazing things. At this point, let me just say that in John's gospel, Chapter 3, Jesus teaches a leader named Nicodemus that a person must be "born again" to see or enter the "Kingdom of God." I don't want to bury you in theology, but Jesus is saying that to have an eternal and personal relationship with Him, and to go to Heaven when you die, you must become a new person from within and follow Him. It is through the power of the "Holy Spirit" that happens. The Holy Spirit is the so-called "third person" of the triune God (Father, son Jesus, and the Holy Spirit). Jesus promised that when He left His earthly ministry, He would send the Holy Spirit to followers of Jesus, and the Holy Spirit would have a ministry including comforting, counseling, and empowering believers.

I mention these deep matters as context at this juncture for a somewhat limited point, but one critical to me. When was I "born again?" The answer is that I don't know for sure, but I have evidence that I was before wild things started happening in Sparta.

Here's my evidence. A fellow who wrote an article about me for a guitar magazine reached out to me later with some spiritual problems he was having. He had lost his faith, or was in danger of losing it. The fact that he reached out to me at all told me something: my faith must have been manifest to him. My response was to make a long cassette recording for him to encourage him in the faith. I can't remember precisely when I did this, whether late in the Mountain Lakes period or early in the Sparta one. In any event, I did the recording with confidence and compassion for him. I simply could not have done it in that spirit without having been "born again." It wasn't a pedagogical exercise; it wasn't lecturing or patting someone on the head and saying "good little boy." It was one Christian brother speaking to another.

I alluded to this event at the end of Chapter 13. It was not technically a "signal of transcendence" but I referred to it in that context because it involved a deep spiritual issue.

37

"There's Something Happening Here"

The words of Stephen Stills from his 1966 hit "For What It's Worth" jump into my head as I start this Chapter. The next line of his song is "what it is ain't exactly clear." That song supposedly arose out of a mob scene in LA in which hundreds of young people protested the imposition of a curfew. That wasn't the situation in Sparta, but I like the flavor of the line. There was indeed "something happening here." Unlike the next line of Stephen's song, it <u>was</u> exactly clear: God was "showing up" in Sparta, NJ.

Sparta was in Sussex County, occupying the far northwestern corner of NJ. The pace was a bit slower than Morris County, where Mountain Lakes was located. A nearby town, Newton, was the County Seat, but Sparta with its population north of 19,000 was an important business center, and had lots of good restaurants, to boot.

After we recovered from our first move in 28 years, we looked around at churches and settled on the First Presbyterian Church of Sparta. It was on a main street in town, called, appropriately, "Main Street." It was about an eight-minute drive from our house on a new development on the side of a hill. Our street was called "Angelo Drive," in honor of one of the sons of the developer, Joe Natale.

Before jumping into the church situation, let me discuss some other outreach Sheila and I did, which had its entertaining aspects.

We assisted the chaplain at a local nursing home. He would hold services on the third floor of the facility, and we would help out. The residents on that floor had some psychological challenges, to say the least. One day the chaplain started to discuss the Book of Jeremiah in the Bible when a lady jumped up and launched into a vigorous if slightly off-key rendition of "Jeremiah was a bull frog!"

For a period of time, I conducted a Bible study on the third floor. While I would be holding forth on some Scripture, a resident would be peacefully asleep right next to me, with his head on the table. I concluded that he was "resting in the Lord" – or at least in some heavy medication.

Back to First Pres (usually pronounced "prez"). The senior pastor there was Tom Litteer, who hailed from Oklahoma and was a wonderful teaching pastor who held the highest view of Scripture and carefully unpacked it. I would occasionally play guitar during the service or at Christmas Eve services. I got to know Tom and his wife Marilyn very well, for reasons you'll soon understand.

Tom was rolling along at First Pres, when something rather dramatic happened to him in March 2005: he got "whacked" (in a good way) by the Holy Spirit. Put another way, he got a Dose of the Ghost.

He was at a mission in Newark, assisting the pastor. People were called for prayer, and Tom went forward expecting to be blessed in a general way. Instead, the man praying over him got a "word of knowledge" about a situation Tom was dealing with. The man knew nothing about the facts, but just got a word from the Lord. Tom was stunned, and fell under the power of the Holy Spirit. That had never happened to him before.

Here are Tom's own words from his doctoral thesis (speaking in the third-person, per that format):

"The next thing the author knew he was on the floor and terribly embarrassed. While he did not hear the audible voice of God, Jesus came to him and told him he loved him. He felt a physical sensation of the love and presence of Jesus that words could not describe.

The author did not attend the lunch, but watched the speaker pray for those who came forward and helped catch them when they fell. What he saw completely captivated him; he had not seen anything like it before. Two hours later, the author asked for another prayer, this time that he might receive the gift of healing. The speaker said it would cost him; he would have to pray for all the sick people he could find. He noted that John Wimber prayed for three thousand people before seeing anyone in his church healed."

The upshot is that Tom brought all this to the church, preached healing and deliverance, and had healing evangelists visit the church and speak. Tom also went on mission trips to Brazil, under the auspices of Rev. Randy Clark's group Global Awakening, based in Mechanicsburg, PA. Not only did he witness healings through others, he himself laid hands on people and in some dramatic cases saw them healed.

That's only the tip of the iceberg for the spiritual trajectory of Tom's life, but it provides a context for me.

I felt the energy at First Pres. Sometimes I walked into the sanctuary before a service and the presence of the Holy Spirit was palpable. The effect was not emotional, but spiritual. There was a "weight" of the glory over the congregation on many occasions.

My involvement with the Holy Spirit came in a more indirect, circuitous way than did Tom's. It started, however, with the miraculous.

On a Saturday in early 2005, I was at a meeting led by a young man who had a healing "anointing" on him. In attendance were a number of people who were faithful church attendees but not so convinced about this healing stuff. The speaker called out people with pain, sickness, or injury, and after a while a spirit of amazement permeated the room. People who had come in there with pains and doubts left the room with neither! There was an atmosphere of wonder in that room.

A man there, Tim, was pursuing pastoral ministry as a second career. The speaker laid hands on him and blessed him. I could tell that Tim, a big, vigorous guy, did not want to fall down under the power of the Spirit. But he did; and he couldn't get up. A year or two later I came right out and asked Tim whether my observation was true, that he didn't want to go down and couldn't get up. He said that not only was it true, but the incident was a significant part of his personal testimony about the power of God acting through the ministry of the Holy Spirit.

A few weeks after that meeting, my wife and I attended a teaching session on evangelism at another church in the area, Lafayette Federated Church. That meeting changed my life in a very unexpected way. I remember nothing of the subject matter, and only two things of a non-substantive nature. First, we used a workbook, my copy of which has gone AWOL. Secondly, the evangelists looked <u>very</u> tired.

As Sheila and I were headed toward the exit at the conclusion of the meeting, we passed a table of evangelistic "product" -- books and other educational materials on the faith. Something on the table caught my eye. It was a plastic package with six CD's in it, representing a distillation of a dialogue between a pastor and a company CEO on the Christian faith that had taken place over many years. It raised questions and offered answers. I bought it.

I challenge anyone to guess how that little package changed my life. Only God could have seen what was going to happen, because He arranged it.

A few days later I sat down and started to go through the discs. I got through all of them, after many hours and days. I started through them <u>again</u>, and spent many <u>more</u> hours and days trying to remember the questions, and trying to remember the answers. It was almost as if I were back in college trying to learn all the right answers to a "Christian Entrance Exam." After the second time through, I took a little break, and then started again.

At the second disc, something amazing happened, which nobody, including me, could have possibly anticipated. As I heard the answer to one question, I was struck with a powerful revelation of the love of God for me. In that respect, my experience parallels Tom's. It was a deep, personal, overwhelming love, and for me. It was not some psychological need that was being met or stroked. It went way beyond that. It was not at its core emotional but spiritual with an emotional consequence, for want of a better description.

In any event, I closed the book on those discs. I ordered a couple of the packages to give to other people, but I had gotten what I needed. That revelation I got in November of 2005 was, I am convinced, my "baptism in the Holy Spirit." My spiritual train hadn't nearly arrived, but it had certainly left the station.

Sometimes you hear preachers say that in the Christian faith, you should preach sin until people get convicted, and then the mercy and grace of God until they get converted. In my case, Tom's case, and that of many other people of faith, it doesn't work that way. Instead, you get a revelation of the love and the glory of God, and that empowers you to deal with sin issues.

Shortly after that experience in 2005, I wrote my testimony down as well as I could. I wanted to have something contemporaneous and in writing, as strong evidence of what happened. I tweaked a few words later for clarity of presentation but not any substance. I offer that testimony below in its entirety.

El Testimony: Beginning in Late 2005

What brought me to a boldness for the Lord was a revelation in late 2005 in four areas:

1. *Understanding the profound love of God for me personally; that God is good all the time; and that any "bad" things that happen come from the "fallen"/sinful state of man or by act of the devil in the world. Put another way, I came to understand and receive the grace and mercy of God in a most personal, direct, and joyful way. That revelation came, interestingly enough, after hours of listening to a CD series (of a Q and A nature) on particular aspects of the Christian faith. I started out by wanting to be informed of Christian responses to questions about the faith. I ended up with the revelation of the love of God.*

2. *Seeing and experiencing miraculous things done by ordinary people in the name of Jesus. That meant healings, deliverance, and other supernatural ways in which the Holy Spirit continues to move among people 2000 years after Christ's earthly ministry and the work of the early church.*

3. *Growing to love and marvel at the written Word of God--the Bible--and at the way in which my life has been transformed by it. It's not simply about getting* information, *but about* transformation; *it's about this wonderful book going directly to the heart and transforming us.*

4. *Growing in faith through increasing confidence in reaching out to the Lord in prayer, and experiencing tremendous breakthrough in answered prayer.*

Those four matters, as I found out later, are great evidence of being "born again", as Jesus taught in John 3:3, and of being "filled with the Holy Spirit," as described in Chapter 2 and elsewhere in the Book of Acts.

A few years after this period, I had more spiritual growth through the revelation of God as our <u>heavenly father</u> who desires constant communication with us and is abundant in His gifts, limited only by (a) any unbelief we have in particular areas of our lives and (b) any immaturity we have at the time (which He will help us work through) in the area of receiving particular blessings He fervently desires to give us.

38

Sister Franny

Having recounted in the previous Chapter the spiritual climate of late November 2005, I need to go back in time with you. Before we can move forward, I need to discuss my sister Franny and share the God-at-work moment involving Franny.

In late 2004, my sister and I visited with her oncologist, and received dreadful news: she had terminal cancer. Her earlier cancer that had been treated and thought to be eradicated, called adenoid cystic carcinoma, had come back in her bones. There was no cure. I remember my sister crying out later, "Why me? What did I do wrong, Sandy?" My answer was, of course, "Nothing, Franny."

She was living in New York City, and I in Sparta. I was going in and out of town regularly, visiting her, handling bills, getting her settled in one hospital, and then what was considered a great hospice in the Bronx. The latter was a mistake, because it made things difficult for Franny's Manhattan church friends to visit her.

Franny's leg collapsed at 5 AM in her New York apartment one morning, and it took 45 minutes before people could hear her cries, break into the room, and take her to the hospital. I wanted to help her, but a snowstorm was raging in the area. I've mentioned the heroic and loyal actions taken by Franny's friends Beverly Bell and Barbara Dunlap, and I mention them again in this context.

Kind people sent Franny scores of Christmas and birthday cards, which remained unopened in December 2004 and January 2005. On February 3, I received a call from the doctor at the hospice confirming that, in his words, "Frances has passed along." (For those people wondering, yes, even at that awful time, I did think of the "day the music died," when Buddy Holly, Ritchie Valens and the "Big Bopper" Richardson died in a plane crash on the same day in 1959.)

During that whole period, I was a physical and emotional wreck. Later that year I was to see healings, and yet earlier in the year the thought never occurred to me to pray or seek divine healing prayer over my sister. I was also concerned that I hadn't paid enough attention to her at the hospice. I saw one case where an attendant was a little harsh with Franny. Was I negligent in taking care of her? I was aware that Franny was solitary by nature. She was sociable, but kept to herself a lot.

At that time of my most agitated state about my sister, the Lord did something miraculous for me. He knew I was starting to beat myself up, and he gave me a "signal of transcendence," as discussed in Chapter 6. As I was gathering Franny's papers together and dealing with the lawyer settling her estate, the Lord drew my attention to a startling fact, a fact that was so significant that it gave me comfort that Franny was with the Lord, and gave me peace about my involvement in her care.

Allow me to share the testimony that I wrote out for our children:

El's Testimony Regarding Frances McMeen And the Love of God

Bob Dylan wrote an amazing song in the late 1970's called "Gotta Serve Somebody." In it he proclaimed that all of us are going to serve somebody. It might be the devil, it might be the Lord, but it would be somebody.

The chorus basically says that we must serve somebody: either God or the devil. I would broaden the devil part to say God, the devil, or the world. Put another way, we serve certain priorities in life. Often, they are work, comfort, health, family, recreation, things like that.

If we view ourselves as serving God first, tremendous blessings will flow from that and affect all aspects of our lives -- family, employment, peace of mind, health, and purpose.

This testimony of mine concerns my sister Fran's death in February 2005, and the aftermath. Fran had been diagnosed with a very rare form of cancer, called adenoid cystic carcinoma of the throat. She was treated by radiation. By all accounts, she was free of the disease after the treatment. She returned to good health and her usual vigor.

A few years later, however, she started having some strange pains in her knees. After a period of months of symptoms and diagnoses, it was discovered that the cancer had come back and was in her bones. I was with her when the oncologist told her the news that it was inoperable. How do you respond to your sister when she cries out to you, "What did I do to deserve this?" The answer I gave was that "you didn't deserve this." (During this period, I did not know anything about prayers for healing, and moving in the miraculous power of God. That happened later in 2005, and intensified thereafter.)

After a period of caretaking in Fran's Manhattan apartment, I had Fran moved to a hospital in Manhattan, and eventually to a hospice in the Bronx. She was treated reasonably well there, but I detected some hardness among the staff. I can imagine the difficulty of working in a place like that.

I received a call on the evening of February 3, 2005, that Fran had "passed along." I remember the words of the doctor.

After that and the rush of funeral preparations and estate matters, I went into a period of great guilt and soul-searching on whether I had done the right things in this whole situation – especially about whether the Hospital in the Bronx was the right place, treated her well, fed her properly and the like.

This is all by way of background, intense and moving as it is. What happened afterwards is what I want to share in particular.

I received Fran's death certificate, which was necessary for certain filings. I looked it over to make sure that it was accurate. It recited that Fran died at 7:40 PM. Some time passed. I was going through Fran's papers, scrapbooks, and other memorabilia. In those materials, I found Fran's birth certificate. More accurately, the Lord led me to that birth certificate.

Why do I say I was "led" to that particular document? I first noted from it that Fran's middle name was spelled with an "s" and not a "z": Elisabeth, not Elizabeth. It was often misspelled in various documents throughout her life. But that was not the reason I was led to that document. I was led to it because of the time that Fran was born.

Fran was born at 7:40 PM, on January 9, 1943. Fran died the very minute that she was born.

What are the chances of that happening? Moreover, what are the chances of my coming across that fact without the guidance of God acting through the Holy Spirit in my life?

I am convinced that the Lord was showing me that, although I didn't and couldn't know the details, there was some kind of plan of God's at work here. He didn't put cancer on Fran; Jesus healed people; He didn't infect people. Yet the fact that I knew He was in this situation gave me peace through this supernatural connecting of the dots of birth and death.

This testimony is one of the most important in my life on the love of God, and his involvement in the details of our lives. This may also be the reason one of my favorite passages of Scripture has an amazing promise in it for believers. It's Philippians 4:6-7:

"Be anxious for nothing, but in everything by prayer and supplication, with thanksgiving, let your requests be made

known to God; and the peace of God, which surpasses all understanding, will guard your hearts and minds through Christ Jesus."

39

What Now?

We now return to November 2005. After my powerful spiritual experience then, the question became what to do? What next? I remember clearly asking the Lord to provide an outlet for my new spiritual energy. I had already read some books by Chuck Swindoll that were helpful in my walk, and I was delving into Scripture much more than I ever had before.

The timing was excellent for charging forward for the Lord. Our children were getting older. All had finished college and were finding their way in law school, grad school, or the workplace. I had retired from touring as a guitarist in the Spring of 2002. I would still do a few performances, record CD's, and write books, but those activities were pretty much within my control.

The first thing I did was finish up my guitar recording "Amazing Grace," containing hymns and spirituals. (Twelve years later I would collect my spiritual music into a double-length recording called "Gospel Guitar Treasures.")

As God would have it, that "Amazing Grace" recording would take me into outreach and apologetics no one could possibly have imagined, involving in the first instance my friend Steve Baughman.

Steve was a great, versatile guitarist who lived in San Francisco. We did three concerts together, two out on the West Coast and one in Virginia. In addition, he was a lawyer who practiced immigration law, and a skeptic on the Christian faith. Having listened to my recording and read the liner notes, he inquired whether we might engage on the Christian faith. I wisely or foolishly said, "Sure!" That was the beginning of what became a furious exchange of e-mails at all hours of the day and night of his attacking, and my defending, the faith. That took place in February 2006.

One grows weary of that type of discussion after a while; at least I did. It can take on somewhat of a "Whack-a-Mole" character. One party asserts proposition A; the other says not-A. Rather than asserting not-not-A, the first party asserts proposition B. The second says not-B, and on and on. I hope you get what I mean.

After two weeks of this I was tired but had the bright idea of pulling the material together as a kind of book. I did that and it was uploaded to the website of the First Presbyterian Church of Sparta. For that, I want to thank then IT guru at the church Dr. David Pontzer, as well as Pastor Dan McEver, who, in an apparent fit of kindly masochism, or masochistic kindness, read the whole thing and discussed it with me.

The piece ran over 100 pages on the website. Steve and I called it the "Passion Dialogues." It has since been taken down, but that's all right. I'm not sure I want to look at it again. I wasn't very spiritually mature at the time. Moreover, it revealed a certain spirit of lawyers posturing and sniping that may have been amusing but not always constructive. Finally, I believe I used in it some example regarding the impossibility of the Chicago Cubs ever winning the World Series again, which God must have enjoyed rendering erroneous in 2016.

That whole episode was a baptism by fire for me. Steve is much more formidable than the usual crowd of critics of the faith. He is aggressive, he has studied the arguments of the Christian and non-Christian apologists, and he has a logical, even brilliant, mind. He is not above being sneaky, cherry-picking verses, and using "straw men," and since I do that, too, I respect it.

Little did we know at the time that we would engage seven years later in another exchange at a much higher and deeper level. It turned into the book referred to in the Foreword to this book. That book, amazingly enough, was funny, too. I'm not sure what runs through Steve's mind when I assert that the God about whom he has doubts or questions used Steve to sharpen <u>me</u> up. Steve may not believe that, but maybe deep down he has a chuckle.

"This book is like a great boxing match! Each contender lands his blows, gets back on his feet, and offers mutual respect. A must-read for anyone serious about real-life issues or the Christian faith."

— Rev. Tony Lee-Mee, Pastor and Co-Director, Rebel Rock Ministry
Website: www.rebelrock.org

"The reader is invited to take a wild ride through an extended discussion between two passionate lawyers. One is a Christian and the other is an Atheist, and they are friends. They do not mince words in sharing their thoughts on the existence of God, heaven and hell, God as just or unjust, miracles, revelation, the Scriptures, and reasonable doubt. Their mutual respect, their ability to articulate their thoughts with razor-like precision, coupled with the fact that such deep discussions between Christians and Atheists rarely take place, make this an intriguing and fascinating read for all with the courage to explore their own assumptions about their faith or non-faith."

— Daniel M. McEvoy, M.Div., Revised Teaching Pastor,
The First Presbyterian Church of Spring, NJ

"What an extraordinary privilege to be allowed to listen in on this conversation of hearts and heads; a conversation that at times spans the cosmos and at times delights in a mischievous smile or a tear of recognition. Any person who has thought deeply about religion has had at least parts of this conversation in his or her head. To have it given voice by accomplished and articulate lawyers is both comforting and provocative."

— Andrew Murray, M.Div., D.Min., Senior Fellow, The Suter Institute
Elizabeth Pence Suter Professor of Peace and Conflict Studies
and Religion (Emeritus) Juniata College, Huntingdon, PA

A must-read on the Christian faith! Not a dry dissertation, but a vigorous, heartfelt dialogue between two thoughtful lawyers and Christians. Passionate, yet humorous; probing, yet breezy. You'll be close along as you ponder deep spiritual matters.

This work also commends itself for Bible studies. Christians appreciate and philosophers, as well as the disciplines of Law, communications, and psychology.

Printed in USA/Australia in Christ

ISBN 978-1-6344-363-9

Objection!
Overruled!

(OR, TWO LAWYERS HAVE A
LITTLE "CHAT" ABOUT GOD AND HELL)

Steve Baughman & Ellsworth McMeen

Objection! Overruled! Steve Baughman and Ellsworth McMeen

40

Rolling Down the Tracts

As I write this book years after the first exchange with Steve, I have weird thoughts, which probably result from writing too much of this book at night. I was baptized by fire, to be sure, but was I broiled, fried, grilled, or sautéed? Moving on.

I wasn't having ridiculous thoughts like the above back in 2006 after the exchange with Steve. I was instead being led by the Lord into a number of other areas of outreach. One involved writing tracts on the faith, in the form of booklets that rarely exceeded in length six folded panels. I'm sure you've seen religious tracts and know what I mean. (If you haven't, please repent and get with the Lord before it's too late.)

If you've managed to finish the previous Chapters on my law practice, you will have some inkling of the miraculous act of God necessary to make me into a tract-writer. I was the guy, after all, who for 28 years as a lawyer in New York was writing dense legal documents that no one ever <u>wanted</u> to read. They had to be written in mind-numbing detail and precision so that if they ever <u>had</u> to be read, by fastidious accountants, lawyers, and judges, they would stand up to scrutiny. To have me, as that guy, writing tracts was almost like using Balaam's donkey to utter prophetic words. (Numbers 22) It was an enormous, divine joke effectuated only through the guiding hand of the Holy Spirit.

I set about writing the little booklets. They almost wrote themselves; seriously. The subjects included: salvation, unforgiveness, contending with worry, humility, love, prayer, prayer not working, rest, and the tongue (and how it gets us into trouble). Writing succinctly and clearly wasn't as much a challenge as I thought it would be (God being there to help me).

It was also fun to play around and format the text into booklets of various types and sizes. I would print out some of the booklets on my home printer; others I would send to a printing company, including the wonderful people at "Moments with the Book" in Bedford, PA. A number of my smaller tracts are contained on their website called "PrintMyTract.com," accessible through the website https://mwtb.org/.

I received confirmation in several ways that whether I knew it or not, God was all over that tract endeavor. One Saturday night I thought I received a "word" that I was to do a tract on "fear." I started typing away. Fairly quickly I got the impression that I should do an Internet search on the subject. What popped up was a Christian book of about 600 pages on the subject of, you guessed it, fear. While looking through the author's table of contents I realized that it was preposterous for me to think I could cover fear in four panels of a booklet. I put my proverbial pencil down, kissed my wife, and turned on the TV in a vain attempt to find something uplifting. I figured "game over" on the tract front that weekend.

God apparently thought otherwise. By the <u>next evening</u>, I had written the tract! But it wasn't on fear. I had the sense that God felt that I simply didn't have sufficient experience with that subject. Believe me, He wasn't saying I was particularly "strong and courageous," to quote the Book of Joshua. Perhaps it was simply that, in His mercy, He had protected me from fear in much of my life. The subject of the tract instead was <u>peace</u>. The title of the booklet was "A Lifestyle of Peace: A Christian Handbook for Maintaining It."

I loved the word "handbook." It connoted something short and handy. I think the Lord gave me that, too. I have a registered trademark on something else that came to me, by Grace no doubt: Pocket Gospel Guide® I did have to figure out how to make that little raised "r" on the computer.

I was busily and happily doing tracts. During one season, I felt called to place them all over Sussex County and elsewhere in all kinds of places legal (or not manifestly illegal), like hospital waiting rooms, stores, and racks in truck stops. (We'll get to truck stops later.)

One time during that period, a church friend of Sheila's presented her with a tract of mine, disheveled-looking and found somewhere in the vicinity of Hardyston, NJ. That was particularly amusing to us because our cat Fritz had papers from the pound indicating that <u>he</u> had been found "wandering around Hardyston." He was amiable but not that sharp of a cat. He probably didn't get too much out of the tract.

After my initial burst of activity on tracts, I had doubts about whether my efforts were bearing fruit. I wasn't getting a lot of feedback. The devil used that as narrative when he would whisper in my ear, "El, you're ineffective and a loser." The Lord helped me smack the devil down, of course, and started to encourage me.

I displayed the tracts at First Pres, and people were picking them up. Rev. Tony Loeffler, who headed up Solid Rock Evangelistic Association, was happy to receive the tracts and use them in his ministry. (More about Tony later.) One time I received an encouraging letter from the relative of an inmate, saying that the inmate had received the tract <u>in</u> prison and sent it to her on the <u>outside</u>. She was blessed, and had to write me to say so.

The Lord used those tracts in other novel ways to bless me. On my way to a guitar get-together in PA, I was going to drop off some tracts at a truck stop by the Delaware Water Gap. (At that time, the owner of the truck stop had racks set aside for Christian materials.) I missed the turn. I said to myself, "Well, I'll do it on the way back." As I was returning from the guitar-fest, however, it started to snow hard. I was tempted not to stop, but, after some circuitous exits and turns, I did.

I was at the truck stop, bearing tracts. I looked all over and couldn't find the racks. Nobody seemed to know where they were. I was walking all over the place, giving off the vibe of someone casing it for a future burglary. I finally found the racks downstairs, around a corner, and against a wall. Voilà! I found a conspicuous place for my tracts, and lined them up.

As I was about to leave, I noticed a CD there by a pastor named Duane Sheriff. Quantities were available on the rack. I took one out of curiosity, and hit the road in the snow.

I found out later that Duane Sheriff was the pastor of a church called Victory Life in Durant, Oklahoma. He had a high-pitched voice and talked fast. He also turned out to be one of the finest teaching pastors I have ever heard. I would go on to listen to, and be greatly edified by, <u>hundreds</u> of hours of his excellent, Bible-based teaching. I even corresponded with him a couple of times.

I honestly believe the Lord was rewarding me for dropping my tracts off at the truck stop. If I hadn't done that, I doubt I <u>ever</u> would have heard of Duane Sheriff, even though he went on to have an internationally acclaimed ministry.

The Lord encouraged me on the tracts in another fascinating way, years later and in a different state. It was 2017, and Sheila and I were living in Huntingdon, PA. (More on that later.) I was at a shop called "Holiday Hair" to have my hair cut. I got talking with the young lady cutting my hair. She attended a church in Three Springs, in southern Huntingdon County. She liked the pastor there, named Denny Hunsinger. I made a mental note of his name.

When I got home, I searched on the Internet for Denny Hunsinger. He was the senior pastor of a church called, of all things, Living Water Christian Outreach. That immediately resonated with me because my previous church, as discussed later in this book, was "Living Waters Fellowship," in Newton, NJ. I thought I detected the hand of the Lord in that one. I wrote Denny a letter, told him about the circumstance with the gal at the hair salon, and included some samples of my tracts.

We got together for breakfast shortly after that, and he told me several things. First, he <u>loved</u> tracts, and used them for years in street ministry. Moreover, when he opened my envelope with the tracts, he had been preparing a sermon. One of the tracts had rocked his world, he told me, and he used it for the sermon! I had brought to that breakfast quantities of the tracts, hoping he would like them. Needless to say, I gave him all those, and a lot more in the future.

One of my tracts is entitled "For the Struggling Christian: Reclaim Your Identity!" In my view, it's the most important tract I've ever written, with the indispensable guidance of the Holy Spirit I believe. It took me, with prodding and hints from the Lord, nearly twelve years to "get it." I include the text in its entirety as the next Chapter. Two other tracts of mine, with minor alterations from the originals, comprise the two succeeding Chapters.

41

For the Struggling Christian: Reclaim Your Identity

As followers of Jesus, we've all had seasons of struggle. If you are in one now, take heart! This little booklet should bless you.

Remember that you are an overcomer; you can stand in the face of attack! Remember also that you do not war against flesh and blood ·· that is, people ·· but against the powers of darkness, Satan and his minions. (Ephesians 6)

<u>Satan's Weapon Exposed</u> Satan's methods are often subtle but can also be somewhat predictable. What he tries to do is this: he will try to steal your Past, your Present, and your Future, by lying to you. That's basically it.

<u>Your Past</u> He tries to obscure your memory of all the wonderful things God has done for you. Remember the Israelites on the other side of the Red Sea? In their frustration, they opened themselves up to the wiles of Satan, who was trying to convince them how good things were on the Egypt side of the Sea! And he tried to make them forget the numerous miracles the Lord had performed for their benefit! (Numbers 11)

<u>Your Present</u> He paints worst-case pictures in your head and tries to convince you they are reality. Or he makes

molehills into mountains in your eyes. Or he points to real mountains, without indicating the paths around them.

Your Future A favorite of the enemy: he tries to steal your hope.

But ... you have hope!

Your Defense

Your first step in resisting the enemy and standing firm in your circumstances is to remember *who you are in the mighty and compassionate triune God!*

Don't let the enemy steal your identity!

The source of the problem when we Christians have struggles in our Christian walk is that the devil, the world, or our flesh has made us lose sight of our *identity* in the triune God – the Father, the Son, and the Holy Spirit. The source of our ability, or privilege, to have an identity in the Trinity is *the shed blood of Jesus Christ on the cross of Calvary.* John 3:14 records the statement of Jesus that He "must" be lifted up – meaning, that His atoning sacrifice for mankind was necessary for the payment of our sins. He came to earth to live a perfect life and then offer Himself a ransom for the many – the finished work of the cross.

Our identity in the triune God

1. Our identity with Yahweh God Jesus taught His disciples to pray "our Father in heaven, hallowed be your name." Our identity with regard to Yahweh is as *beloved adopted sons and daughters of our Father,*

the King, to whom we have access 24/7. As we grow in that identity, we become less likely to blame God for the bad things, and more likely to move in our identity as beloved children of a caring God. A good father, to be sure, must discipline his children, but he uses the least amount of force necessary for correction.

2. Our identity with Jesus There are several aspects, but let's focus on two of them:

   a. John 15: Jesus is the true vine, God is the vine-dresser, and we are the branches. To the extent that we remain attached to Jesus, we remain strong branches, and wonderful fruit happens. Jesus tells us that apart from Him we can do nothing. The critical area is the junction where the branch is attached to the vine. We all have areas of hardness there (like sap from a tree that becomes hardened, or scar tissue). Those beliefs, actions, or attitudes include unforgiveness, ungodly anger, unbelief, pride, envy, fear, distraction, and the like. That hardness produces two bad results: we become detached from Jesus and attached to the hardness, and the health of the branch suffers, as does the fruit. The solution is not gritted-teeth determination so much as attending to "tenderizing" the attachment to Jesus, through worship, praise, gratitude, and faith creating a welcoming environment for the Father to "prune" the hardness through the ministry of the Holy Spirit.

b. <u>Epistles of Paul</u>: <u>Each of us is a member of the body of Christ, with Jesus as head</u>. We aren't to envy the gifts of others, nor to believe that we have to do everything ourselves. We aren't to go "Lone Ranger" and believe that it's all about our individual relationship with God, apart from the church. The Christian faith is a "team game."

3. <u>Our identity with the Holy Spirit</u> We are the beloved beneficiaries of "the positive ministry of the Holy Spirit." (Thanks to Andrew Wommack for the quoted term.) The Holy Spirit is our comforter and our counselor; He guides us into all truth, and provides words for us when we are at a loss; He intercedes for us when we don't have the words in our prayers to the Father; He empowers us; and He searches the deep things of God. How often we Christians ignore the yearnings of the Holy Spirit to help us! He is in us, through us, beside us, ahead of us, and behind us. Although the Holy Spirit does not convict the believer of sin, nevertheless, he guides us into all truth, and one of those truths may well be identifying particular sins in our lives that are entangling, ensnaring, or enslaving us! He will then help us escape the bondage of those sins – IF we go to him, ask, and listen for and heed the answer.

<u>Conclusion</u> The devil tries to steal our past, our present, and our future, and he is also interested in stealing our identity. When we are engaged in struggle with him, or the wiles of the world, or the weakness of our flesh, it's amazing how simply reflecting on our identity in the triune God is

liberating, and empowers us to marshal the weapons we believers have to defeat the works of the enemy.

As a follower of Jesus, you are an overcomer!

Black and white picture of stained
glass artwork by Dee Turba.

42

Are We Sure That We Are Right With God?

Romans 3:23 confirms that:

"All [of us] have sinned and fall short of the glory of God."

We try to do the right thing; we try to think the right thoughts. But how often we fail! When we consider the holiness of Almighty God, we realize, and the Bible confirms, that we cannot earn or work our way into a healthy and peaceful relationship with God! Pretending that God doesn't exist, or ignoring the fact that some day we must account to God for our actions and thoughts, is not the answer.

So, then, what do we do?

Ephesians 2:8-9 tells us:

"For by grace you have been saved through faith, and that not of yourselves; it is the gift of God, not of works, lest anyone should boast."

There is only one way to "get right" with God: it is by getting to know Jesus, and placing our faith in Him, rather than continuing to "do life" in our own strength and for our own purposes.

This requires shedding our adult pride that says "I'll do what I want!" Instead, we must approach this subject humbly with a child-like trust in the path God has set before us for our own good. God is our Father and Creator; He knows what's good for us. Our past hurts and disappointment can be obstacles to our doing this, but we must persevere. A tremendous gift awaits us if we do.

John 3:16 tells us that we can have eternal life -- that is, a close and personal relationship with God, now and forever:

"For God so loved the world that He gave His only begotten Son, that whoever believes in Him should not perish but have everlasting life."

God desires to have intimacy with us, in every detail of our lives. He, moreover, has provided a helper to us. The Holy Spirit is the comforter and counselor who lives inside every believer. We mature over time through the Holy Spirit, as we hear and meditate on the word of God (the Bible), and as we praise and worship God and speak with Him freely and honestly in prayer.

James 4:8 contains God's promise to us:

"Draw near to God and He will draw near to you. Cleanse your hands, you sinners; and purify your hearts, you double-minded."

As to any "good works" that we may do, Ephesians 2:10 confirms that good works are the <u>fruit</u> or result of a saving faith in Jesus, not the <u>root</u> or means of getting right with God:

"For we are His workmanship, created in Christ Jesus for good works, which God prepared beforehand that we should walk in them."

Intimacy with God: ABC Issues of the Heart

We must:

<u>A</u>cknowledge that we have done wrong and hurtful things in thought and action ("sin").

<u>B</u>elieve in Jesus for the forgiveness of our sins and for eternal life.

"He who believes in the Son has everlasting life; and he who does not believe the Son shall not see life, but the wrath of God abides on him." (John 3:36).

<u>C</u>onfess Jesus as our Savior and Lord, and turn toward Him and away from our sins.

"... if you confess with your mouth the Lord Jesus and believe in your heart that God has raised Him from the dead, you will be saved." (Romans 10:9).

El tract.

43

Unforgiveness: A Christian Guide to Tearing Down That Wall

Unforgiveness in our lives is a stronghold. It is a fortress. It is a wall around our mind, our heart, and our body. It keeps us in bondage. It keeps us in torment.

We build it stone by stone because someone has hurt us. Someone has offended us. It was real. It hurt.

And we can't let it go.

This little pamphlet, together with your meditation on it, your prayers, and help from the Holy Spirit in your life, can lead you to victory over unforgiveness.

Jesus said (John 10:10):

"The thief does not come except to steal, and to kill, and to destroy. I have come that [you] may have life, and ... have *it* more abundantly."

Forgiveness and Unforgiveness

Forgiveness of another means releasing that person's responsibility to us for a grievance we have against that person, and giving up to God the whole situation.

Forgiveness does not mean "trust". Forgiveness is given; trust must be earned.

Unforgiveness in our lives leaves us in a state of anxiety, even torment, and limits our ability to have our prayers heard and answered by God. It also keeps us from receiving the full benefit of the "fruit of the [Holy] Spirit," including love, joy, peace, patience, and self-control. (Galatians 5:22-23)

Unforgiveness is a "stronghold" in our minds and hearts. That means a fortress or castle that <u>we</u> have built by our thoughts and emotions, usually over time. It must be pulled down. We must address the problem with an attitude of humility, so we will use the words "Be Humble" as our key to do this.

Be Humble

<u>B</u> <u>Bible</u>. Jesus commands us to forgive those who offend or hurt us. The Lord's Prayer links God's forgiveness of us to our forgiveness of others: "forgive us our debts, <u>as we</u> <u>forgive</u> our debtors" (Mt 6:12) Jesus also requires our forgiveness as a condition to having our prayers answered. (Mark 11:24-27). The Bible provides guidance to us in <u>overcoming</u> unforgiveness. That's the basis of this outline.

<u>E</u> We must strive for a lifestyle of <u>Encouragement</u>. It's easier to criticize, to lecture, and to correct someone, but encouragement is the way to victory for us and for the other person. (A great example of encouragement in the Bible is Barnabas, in the Book of Acts. He was a "good man.")

H <u>Humility</u>. We must approach the subject of unforgiveness in our lives from the standpoint of <u>humility</u> and searching for truth, and not pride. Proverbs 15:33 teaches us:

"The fear of the LORD *is* the instruction of wisdom, And before honor *is* humility."

U <u>Understanding</u> the stronghold of unforgiveness. It is a fortress in our minds, which threatens to wall off our soul (mind, emotions, and will) and our body from the cleansing power of the Holy Spirit in us. We ourselves have built it, usually rock by rock over time.

Here's how it happens: an offense to us leads to negative thoughts; then, we become mentally and emotionally invested in those thoughts. We start to elevate them in importance in our character. Eventually our pride dominates the situation and we can become hostile to correction and to the truth. (2 COR 10:4-5). Negative strongholds like unforgiveness are the devil's playground. He can play on our anger, and other negative thoughts and emotions, and bring us down.

M Renewal of our <u>Mind</u> is the method for overcoming unforgiveness. (Romans 12:2) We must pursue a lifestyle of thinking about our thoughts. We must bring our thoughts "into captivity" to obedience to Christ. (2 COR 10:5)

That involves <u>repentance</u> -- confession (with our mouths) of the stronghold we have; <u>changing our minds</u>; and <u>changing our direction</u> in the area. That action empowers us (1) to identify how the devil tries to work in our minds and (2) to bind him and cast him out in the name of Jesus!

By thinking about our thoughts, we can better resist any temptation to add new rocks to a stronghold. We do this by approaching hurts and wrongdoing towards us, not as a reason for offense, but instead as an opportunity for us to contend against unforgiveness by tearing down strongholds and not building them up. That approach will lead to validation of our own growth in the Lord in this area. The validation is evidenced by increased <u>peace</u> in our lives.

<u>B</u> <u>Blood of Jesus</u>, shed for our sins. We must keep things real. Whatever our problems are, Jesus lived a sinless life and yet laid it down for all sinners. Our grievances can't compare to that act of mercy and salvation. We should focus on Him. (Philippians 4:8) Moreover, we can "plead the Blood" as a defense against the enemy's accusations and attempts to make us feel worthless by reason of our failings in the area of unforgiveness.

<u>L</u> <u>Let</u> our Christian brothers and sisters help us out in the area of unforgiveness. By exchange of testimonies, we can build up each other's faith. We must be careful, however, not to let sympathetic responses from our friends reinforce or add to any stronghold of unforgiveness!

<u>E</u> The apostle Paul told his student Timothy that Timothy had to "<u>exercise</u>" himself for the purpose of godliness. (1 Timothy 4:7) We have to practice in the area of unforgiveness, with prayers for wisdom from God, with heartfelt repentance when we fail, and with continual reaching out for the assistance of the Holy Spirit.

Unforgiveness is a wall in our mind. We have built it

stone by stone. It keeps the power of the Holy Spirit from cleansing our soul and our body. It keeps us in torment.

<u>We must tear it down to gain Victory.</u>

Unforgiveness

*A Christian Guide To
Tearing Down That Wall*

Pocket Gospel Guide Series® No. 4
El McMeen

44

God Likes Thumb Picks: Rev. Tony Loeffler and the Solid Rock Evangelistic Association

My friend Mark Breckenridge from Sparta knew I played guitar, and thought I might enjoy meeting a minister friend of his, Tony Loeffler. Rev. Tony was a New Jersey guy who had relocated to Florida. He had in his youth experienced the world of drugs, pain, and incarceration. Redeemed by the power of God operating through the Holy Spirit, Tony established and ran an organization called Solid Rock Evangelistic Association that focused on prison ministry and evangelism, in the US and abroad.

I remember several things from his first visit at my house. First, we hit it off big-time. Secondly, I advocated his using a thumb pick for his guitar-playing. He later told me it changed his life in music. (Readers who are musicians know that this kind of thing can happen.) Third, he was a cool-looking dude, with annoyingly good hair, and reminded me of Johnny Cash. I found out later how much he sounded like Johnny and liked his music. Lastly, his ministry could always use contributions. (Hint, hint. Go online and help him out.)

Tony and his team of volunteers would go into prisons, primarily but not exclusively in Florida, and play spiritual music of different genres, including southern gospel, jazz, and blues. He would preach and teach the gospel of Jesus Christ, pray over inmates for healing and deliverance from demonic oppression, and make altar calls for their salvation. In later years, he and his colleagues would develop a program, with extensive and impressive materials, to create and equip the "Church Behind Bars." Such church would be self-sustaining, with the help of God, and not dependent on teaching from outside speakers.

Tony's problem then was that although his work in the prisons was very fruitful, he lacked the time and manpower to follow up with inmates who wrote him long letters with serious concerns. He could handle routine requests for Bibles and materials, but couldn't counsel inmates. I'm not a counselor, either, but I volunteered to help take the load off Tony regarding inmates who needed more attention.

The result of this was my correspondence with over a hundred inmates, through hundreds of letters exchanged over nine years, and counting. The letters going out and coming in could be long, detailed, and deep, as inmate doubts, anger, and despair had to be countered with the love of God. That sometimes took "tough love." I also kept in touch with a number of men who had been released.

It was amazingly rewarding at times and frustrating at other times. I developed some rules of thumb, or intuition, on when I was being manipulated or "played." Conversely, I had to make sure I wasn't becoming hardened or cynical, quick to jump to negative conclusions about an inmate's motivations.

Tony also introduced me personally to men who were in prison or who had been. Sometimes they were notorious. We don't have to get into specifics, but there were some household names among them.

Tony and I became dear friends. We speak often on the phone, and don't hesitate to seek or offer prayer on the spot. I was struggling with a breathing problem in 2014, having been up three nights straight virtually without sleep. I asked for a prayer of deliverance against what I discerned were demonic forces at work. Tony dropped everything he was doing to pray over me by phone. As soon as he did, I felt a substantial weight come off me, and that night I was able to sleep in a chair until 4 AM, which was a massive breakthrough. The next night I slept through the night in bed. I know that he, too, can boast in the Lord as to breakthroughs that have happened in his life after our prayers. They were in areas of improved health, doors being opened for fulfilling ministry, and prophetic words and signs.

Finally, I want to thank Tony for introducing me to the ministry of two fine young people in England, Jonathan and Heather Bellamy, who are part of the U.K. media ministry at crossrhythms.co.uk/. Over the years I have written many articles for that website, accessible at this URL:

http://www.crossrhythms.co.uk/articles/life/?author=13476

You can meet Him before that, in the person of
the Holy Spirit, but I still like the sign.

45

Ministry in Newton: Towers and Waters

The title of this Chapter may sound like the name of a law firm, but it's my way of capsulizing two very important places for me. The word "towers" refers to an apartment building called "Brookside Terrace" in Newton, NJ, the County Seat of Sussex County. The word "Waters" is shorthand for "Living Waters Fellowship" in Newton.

Brookside Terrace

Brookside Terrace is the formal name, but people in Newton tend to call it "the high-rise," since it stands out in town as a ten-story building. Brookside has garden apartments, too, but will always be "the high-rise."

First Pres had a ministry to the residents of Brookside. The church contributed computers to the Brookside "community room," and church members participated in various activities there. They worked with Brookside's dedicated, thoughtful, and energetic Director of Social Services, Virginia Shamlian. First Pres Pastor Tom Litteer for a season even conducted worship services in the community room, with music provided by members of the worship team. Jan Pontzer spent five years at Brookside fellowshipping with residents over knitting.

First Pres people weren't the only ones to help out at Brookside. Pastor Budd Brown faithfully served at the high-rise for many years on a weekly basis, teaching, playing worship music on his Martin guitar, and administering Communion in the community room.

After I attended a church service at Brookside in 2006, I found myself wondering whether I had anything to offer over there. I talked with Tom, who told me to talk with Virginia and go for it. Before I even knew what was happening, I found myself in Virginia's office broaching the idea of a weekly Bible study. Virginia gave me some papers explaining "Section 8 housing" and the U.S. Department of Housing and Urban Development ("HUD"). We agreed to think about it.

That discussion turned into a weekly Bible-based "fellowship group" that met every Thursday morning. It started in early September 2006 and lasted until the end of June 2012. There were a few gaps when I was unavailable (for example, when I was dealing with my mother's house and estate after she died in 2007). But the group became a fixture at Brookside.

A sister in Christ, Lisa Schwarz, attended the meetings and was very helpful to the group and me. Among other things, Lisa introduced me to the ministry of Andrew Wommack, whose teaching and materials have been a real blessing to me and have equipped me in my own walk with the Lord. The group was comprised primarily of mature women, and Lisa helped me understand the "mindset" of some of them. I was a guy, and could be relatively clueless about was going on beneath the surface of the meetings sometimes.

Although I had led sessions on the famous "third floor" of the nursing home, I had never before facilitated in any systematic way a "small group." Some decisions had to be made regarding the place for the meeting, whether it should be open or closed, and what the "vibe" should be. Would I make a formal presentation each week (preaching/teaching) or should it be more free-form?

Virginia had a Master's Degree in a discipline that included small groups. She was very familiar with their dynamics and provided invaluable assistance in our effort to make the group "work."

I insisted that the group be Bible-based. I didn't want to use other resources and then have someone argue, "Well, that may work for <u>you</u> but not for <u>me</u>." Virginia and I decided to have the group function in the open in the community room, so that curious people might be drawn in. Virginia turned off the TV during sessions, and we asked people in the room to be quiet, to avoid distractions.

We didn't have any set "curriculum." I would simply choose topics as I felt led by the Lord during the twenty hours or so per week I spent in preparation for each meeting. That time of preparation for Brookside provided some of my most important education in the faith. Moreover, our study and discussion at the group would lead to one of my early tracts, from 2007, called "Hard Times: A Christian Handbook for Getting Through Them." That brochure went through several printings and has been widely disseminated. It is a tall "rack brochure," with a brown cover, and reflects some fine design work by a Montana printing company, PrintingCenterUSA.

At the first meeting of the group I passed out hardbound NIV Bibles, so that everyone would have a personal copy. As I settled into the weekly pace of the meetings, I began to focus on the aesthetics of the materials I provided. I wanted them to be excellent, just as our Lord is excellent. I wanted each Bible text I handed out to be striking, in color or on colored paper, or accompanied by a picture or some other artwork.

Later on, I had the idea that it would be nice to give out notebooks, so that each person could have in an accessible and portable place the material for each week. I didn't want the notebooks to be too big or clunky. Some people were in wheelchairs or used canes to walk, and had enough to worry about. I found the solution: a little plastic box containing plastic sleeves for CD's, very much like the box of CD's that had earlier changed my life! I bought a quantity of those boxes and plastic sleeves, and gave them out to the group. I made sure the materials I passed out would fit into those CD sleeves.

I'm looking at my own plastic box now. It really takes me back. There is a sheet, inside the plastic cover, that reads "Brookside Terrace Fellowship Group: Scriptures for Life." Below that on the left are the words "This is My Book," followed by a line on which people could write their names. (I have "El" written on mine.) At the upper left is a picture of Brookside. I counted the number of sheets of paper in mine, and the total is 39! As I look through the pages, I'm making a promise to myself to keep that little notebook on my desk, and go through those materials again. It's like my personal mini-Bible. I hope other members of the group treasure their copies, too.

The size of the group would vary each week, depending on what was going on at the high-rise, absences due to necessary doctor appointments, and the like. Sometimes we would watch Christian movies or have open discussions. Other times we would be caught up in a tragedy or trauma at the high-rise and discuss sickness, death, and other events affecting members of the group. It may seem cold, but I had to make sure that tragedy and drama didn't dominate the discussions. A spirit of victimhood or boredom in some quarters of the group, if unchecked, could turn every problem into a crisis.

As the years passed, I became more relaxed, less obsessive in preparation, and more comfortable in my role at Brookside. When I started in 2006, I felt driven to try to anticipate every conceivable question and concern that might be raised. As it was, even at the end of my tenure there, my blood pressure was elevated 20-30 points over my normal level. I know that because nurses would periodically come to Brookside to take blood pressures. I, of course, with my warped sense of humor, accused my group members of trying to kill me.

Brookside was one of the most important Christian experiences of my life. It was often very trying, dealing with some deep-seated issues of anger, unforgiveness, and depression among group participants. They were a bunch of survivors of some awful stuff that had taken place in their lives -- typically abuse, rejection, or abandonment, or all the foregoing. As a result, many of our people harbored serious unforgiveness.

One time I drew the group's attention to the so-called "Love Chapter," 1 Corinthians, Chapter 13, and a verse in the NIV translation. Verse 5 says that love "keeps no record of wrongs." Uh, oh. Some of my group members really didn't like that one, since a favorite activity was trotting out their lists of the various offenses perpetrated on them in the past.

The group could also be great fun. The Holy Spirit was always at work there. Even on days when I encountered darkness as soon as I walked into the building, the atmosphere would invariably change during the course of the meeting, and hope would break through. Praise God.

Living Waters Fellowship

Tom Litteer, as described earlier, was experiencing the power of the Holy Spirit in a real and personal way. Even though he had been at First Pres in Sparta for over fourteen years, he felt a fresh anointing and brought that passion to the church. Not everyone there, however, was feeling the joy. Moreover, the national governing body of the Presbyterian Church in the USA ("PCUSA") was in a process of compromising on certain social issues and straying from Biblical principles.

After much prayerful consideration, Tom felt a strong call to establish a new, independent church to serve the residents of Newton. A number of us at First Pres were drawn to that initiative, having ourselves experienced healing, deliverance, and boldness for the Lord and wanting to grow in the power of the supernatural.

The new church was given the name "Living Waters Fellowship." The nine original Trustees and Elders were, in addition to Tom and his wife Marilyn, Keith and Connie

Keoppel, David and Jan Pontzer, Nick and Cathy Boon, and myself. Sheila was busy on various fronts at First Pres, and remained there.

I worked with Tom and the church's helpful outside counsel, Henry King and Lisa Albright of the Reed Smith law firm, on organizational matters. David Pontzer handled the website, and he and I worked on the uploading of many of my tracts.

Elder Keith Keoppel and I worked with Tom to find a suitable venue for our church services. Sussex County Community College was gracious enough to provide, for a small fee, space at a concert hall on campus. It served the church very well until the church moved to 93 Spring Street in downtown Newton, to a space previously occupied by a bank. "From Loans to the Lord," we would quip.

I recall with great pleasure the activities that took place on August 1, 2009, the day before our first church service. It said so much about the different gifts and talents needed for the church to run. David Pontzer was in the hall dealing with sound issues. I was there thinking through the music that would grace the service the next day. I was also trying to figure out how the lighting worked. I was having real trouble with one lighting panel. (It would take me a couple months to realize that the panel simply didn't work.) Finally, David's wife Jan was doing the really important stuff. She was walking around the room, praising God, blessing the church, and praying in tongues.

It's too early to write the book on Living Waters as a new church with energy and challenges, walking out its mission of doing the Lord's work in the world. I will say this: the experience at Living Waters brought into bold relief the monumental wisdom packed into one verse from the first epistle of Paul to the Thessalonians, 1 Thessalonians 1:5:

"... our gospel did not come to you in word only, but also in power, and in the Holy Spirit and in much assurance, as you know what kind of men we were among you for your sake."

That verse, amazing in its brevity and fullness, captures what I believe are the six necessary elements of an effective local body. They are:

1. the church must be all about the <u>full gospel</u> of Jesus Christ, nothing less;

2. the gospel must be preached in <u>words</u>;

3. the gospel must be experienced and practiced in <u>action, in the supernatural power of God</u>;

4. the church must be constantly grateful for, welcoming to, and in sold-out partnership with, the <u>Holy Spirit</u>;

5. a spirit of <u>confidence in the Lord</u> must permeate the church; and

6. the <u>leadership must model our Lord</u>, while acknowledging human frailty. The leaders must not, in any event, be captive to any known, habitual, and unrepented sin.

46

"There's Something Strange, In the Neighborhood"

I love the movie "Ghostbusters." I saw it at least ten times in movie theaters. Things got so bad by the sixth or seventh time that if I was with a friend, I would be blurting out and laughing at the upcoming lines. Some perceptive person once identified the crux of Bill Murray's humor. He was manic when the situation called for calm, and calm when the situation called for mania.

By no means do I want to trivialize by the "Ghostbusters" reference what I am going to share with you. But there was "something strange in the neighborhood," and it was Mr. El's Neighborhood.

If you know me personally, you know that I'm not exactly the poster child for weird flights of fancy. If you know me only through this book, you may question (properly, I admit) my sense of humor and misspent youth, but there isn't sufficient evidence to deem me a whacko. That having been said, let me share with you some strange things. For ease of reference, I will create sub-headings.

The Strange Case of the Psalms

In 2005-6 I worked with a couple of guitarist friends to produce their CD. The friends were Sandy Shalk and Tim Alexander and their recording on the Piney Ridge Music label is called "Giving Voice." (Buy it; it's great.)

After working with the guys all day, I was wired, and got up at 3:30 the next morning at the hotel. What should pop into my head at that hour was "Psalm 150." That was it. Psalm 150. That was strange. I never in my life had <u>read</u> Psalm 150. I found a Bible, turned to Psalm 150, and read the following in verses 1 and 3-5:

1 Praise the Lord!...

3 Praise Him with the sound of the trumpet;
Praise Him with the lute and harp!

4 Praise Him with the timbrel and dance;
Praise Him with stringed instruments and flutes!

5 Praise Him with loud cymbals;
Praise Him with clashing cymbals!

Now that was something. I spent the whole previous day producing guitar tracks, and the Lord gave me a Psalm that mentioned stringed instruments!

But it didn't stop there. It happened for the next few days. I would have a thought, and a Psalm number would come to me; then another thought, and another Psalm number. <u>They were always on point</u>.

Then Psalm 88 came to me. It dealt with dark stuff, wrath, and death, "lowest pit" here, "abomination" there. I frankly didn't get it. I even looked at Psalms 87 and 89 to see whether God made a typo in the download to me (just kidding, Lord). The puzzle remained for a few days.

Then came church. Pastor Tom was talking about an inmate he had been writing. I was listening casually, taking it in generally, until he said something that really made my ears perk up. The inmate had Psalm 88 tattooed on his leg! Psalm 88. The one I couldn't figure out.

The Strange Case of 7's and 11's

Then there was the situation involving the numbers 7 and 11. Let me quote extensively from my article for Cross Rhythms, appearing at this URL:

http://www.crossrhythms.co.uk/articles/life/Rolling_The_Spiritual_Dice/23739/p1/

Sometimes we think about life as a roll of the dice, don't we? Since gambling odds are never very good, we tend to think that way when the dice come up "snake eyes" - or some other unlucky combination.

Well, consider this!

The numbers 7 and 11 are lucky numbers, right? Not being much of a gambler, I don't know all the details, but I know that these numbers mean good things for the gambler. You get one or both; you win.

Here's where things get interesting for me. Over the years, I have begun to notice that in times of stress the numbers 7 and/or 11 have begun to appear to me. They have shown up in a variety of fascinating ways - divine reassurance and comfort.

When I feel pressured, and look around for the numbers, they aren't there. I can't conjure them up when I want them. They always come as a surprise! I kid you not.

For example, in literally scores of instances when I have been apprehensive about something, I've glanced at the clock, and the time has been 7:11...or 11:11...or 7:07...or 11:07.

There are 1,440 minutes in the day. The chances of looking up and seeing some 7/11 time represent roughly .006--or, in words, point 6 percent. Talk about odds!

Was I somehow "programming" myself so that I would instinctively look at the clock at certain times of the day? That may sound plausible, but consider the following.

I was scheduled to give a guitar concert in Denver, Colorado a few years ago. I arrived there exhausted. Perhaps worse, my guitar didn't take well at all to the dry air out there. In the hotel room the night before the concert, I was struggling. I practiced my pieces, and was desperately adjusting the guitar setup so that the darned thing wouldn't buzz. In the middle of this, I glanced at the clock in the hotel room. It said 7:11. Boy, did that calm me down. The concert went very well the next day.

Now, if my body somehow programmed me to look at the clock then, it was pretty smart to factor in the two-hour time difference between NJ and Denver! I don't think so.

Or consider this: one time I was extremely apprehensive about the quality of some recording I had done. I was listening to the demo CD on a portable disc player. I glanced at the player, and it showed the elapsed time as 7:11! Think of the odds. In that case, if I had looked at the player one SECOND later, it would have shown 7:12, since the 11 represented seconds not minutes. How about that-- pretty amazing, no?

Another time I was worried about something while I was listening to the Discman. I glanced at the player. It showed that I was listening to Track 7, and that 11 seconds had elapsed in the track--7-11 again!

This 7-11 phenomenon goes beyond time. A number of years ago, on very short notice, I was asked to go to Maine, and address a major client on a complicated legal issue. As I was sweating things out in my hotel room, I noticed my room number --117. The numbers 11 and 7 to the rescue!

But there's more: I was booked to do a guitar concert at perhaps the premier club on the West Coast--with the unlikely name of the Freight and Salvage, in Berkeley, California. I worried about that show night and day for three weeks before I did it. As it turned out, it went well. Only when I got home after the show, and started to recover my strength, did I notice that the club's address in Berkeley was...1111 Addison Street!

Just one more of these...on more than one occasion in church, when I have been in a troubled state of mind, the Scripture lesson has been chapter 7, starting at verse 7 or 11, or chapter 11, verse 7 or 11. One of my favorite miracles of Jesus turns out to begin at Luke 7:11 - the raising of the son of the widow of Nain.

Have you experienced something similar? I bet you have. We tend to think of God in Old Testament terms of power and force, or New Testament terms of love and comfort...but He also clearly has a sense of humor! After all, if He didn't, how could WE have one? And what better way to manifest it to us humble, flawed human beings than at times when we need comfort and support?

After I wrote all of this, I mused with my son Jon about whether I had jinxed myself and never would see 7-11 again. Putting this issue out of my mind and needing some information for tax purposes, I began to rummage through some closing papers from 1975 on our previous home. As my eye was casually running through a mortgage statement from back then, I handed the paper to my son, and asked him to look at my monthly obligation for mortgage and real estate taxes. We both roared with delight; the number was $711.

Just so you know, I had not seen 7's and 11's for several years until recently, as I am writing this book! In the last few days I saw the time 7:11 four times. I'm thinking that maybe the Lord is pleased with this book!

The Strange Case of a "Word of Knowledge"

One Wednesday I decided to take a ride to the truck stop at the Delaware Water Gap and put some tracts out. It was a nice day, and I was driving on the usual route of 94 South past Blairstown and down to the truck stop.

On the way I got the distinct impression that I was to pray for healing of someone's neck. There was a nice lady at the counter next to the tract racks, so I figured she was the one. I got to the truck stop, went to the rack area, but she wasn't there. I put my material in the rack, left, and drove home.

The next day was Brookside. We had a good meeting, and right before we were to break up I remembered the word about necks. I asked whether anyone at the table had a sore neck. One lady did. I prayed over her neck in the name of Jesus. Afterwards, she felt much better. That was encouraging.

Time passed, and I made another trip to the truck stop and took tracts for the rack. This time the lady was there. I had never really spoken with her before, and was a little hesitant at first. I told her the story about the word about the neck, and looking for her, and she wasn't there, etc. She looked at me and said, "I had a bad neck problem, and now it's gone. Thank you for praying for me."

How about that! But here's the thing: I never really prayed for her specifically. Something must have happened in the heavenlies in connection with that whole episode.

But there's more: the next time I went to the truck stop, she was gone, her desk was gone, and there was some kind of machine where you grab stuff with a metal claw. I never saw that lady again. Never. Oh, by the way, guess what her name was. It was "Angela" – as in Angel with an a. The Bible tells us there are angels among us. I'm just saying.

The Strange Case of Cardinals, Lights, and Horns

With my legal training I'm big on getting confirmation of things, especially if I think I'm getting a word from the Lord on something. When I later share with you what happened in connection with our move to Huntingdon, you'll see more of that.

I was getting deeper and deeper into Scripture and time with the Lord. I would receive in fascinating ways confirmation of thoughts I was having. I start with the cardinal.

Our house in Sparta had a den that was a really comfortable place for me to read the Bible, listen to sermons on a portable disc player, and get with the Lord in prayer. Outside the window was this cardinal. He would chirp in the way they do. I would look out, but I never could see him. I looked everywhere, craning my neck into a pretzel, and still couldn't see him.

One day I was grappling with the apparent contradiction in the Bible between Paul and James on the subject of good works. Paul clearly says we are saved by grace, through faith, and not by works, because we could brag about them. James emphasizes works. There is Bible language, such as

James 2:24, that if you wanted to make trouble about the faith, you could. Martin Luther's solution was to yank James out of the Bible. Mr. Luther was great on many issues, but not that one.

The usual way of harmonizing Paul and James is to say that we are saved by the grace of God, through faith alone, but to add that faith is <u>never</u> alone. It is always accompanied by good works of some sort. But there is still that pesky language in James 2:24.

I was thinking about all this. After a while the thought occurred to me that the problem was in the use of the word "faith." Paul was talking about faith as a deep commitment of the soul, and James was really talking about "head knowledge."

The moment I had that thought, the cardinal that had been MIA for a month flew past the window. I kid you not. I considered that as validation that I was at least on the right track with Paul and James.

After that experience I would routinely see a cardinal right after I had some spiritual thought. It might be a revelation of some sort, or an application of Scripture to something I was doing, or an encouragement to follow through on something I was going to do. I would be driving and a cardinal would fly across the road, right after I mused about something, or I'd hear the distinctive chirp of a cardinal right after a thought flashed in my mind.

A skeptic might interrogate me and ask, "Well, didn't you see a cardinal when you weren't having deep thoughts?" The answer is that if I did, that fact had no impact on me. I can't remember. We are talking about the facts, to be sure, but also the impact.

I like to get with the Lord early in the morning – sometimes 3 or 4 AM. I might listen to a sermon and have a thought on theology or application of the sermon to a particular person or situation, and something would immediately happen to confirm that. In Sparta, it would tend to be the lights of a car going down Angelo Drive. Later in Huntingdon, the signal would be a train whistle. Back in Sparta now, it's the car lights again in the dead of night.

But there is a new one now. When I am with the Lord in the middle of the night, the little green light on the cable box goes off and on, completely beyond my control. It seems to go on right after I have a thought about some spiritual matter. I can't make this stuff up

Dealing with the Weather

The earlier parts of this Chapter are a warm-up for what I want to share now. Hold on to your hats. We are going to address the issue of controlling the weather through the power of God through faith.

Mark 4:35-41 contains the account of Jesus "calming the storm," as some people like to say. Right off the bat, that's wrong. Jesus didn't "calm the storm." He rebuked the storm. A demonic force had come against the boat, and that power had to yield to the power of Jesus. After Jesus did that, he turned to the disciples and questioned their faith. You can preach that dramatic event in all kinds of different ways, but I like the Charismatic approach holding that

Jesus was telling the disciples that <u>they</u> should have been the ones to rebuke the wind in the power of God.

I've tried maybe five times actually to muster up the faith to control the weather in the mighty name of Jesus. I want to share them all with you, to build your faith, confess my own inadequacy, and show you some divine humor.

One time I ordered the rain to stop, in the name of Jesus, and nothing happened. That actually happened after the other events I'll recount. I wanted to start with it to show you an example of my abject failure in faith.

The first time I went after the weather involved a massive rainstorm in Sparta. I got tired of it, was revved up in faith, took authority in Jesus's name, and commanded the sun to come out. Guess what happened. Shortly after that prayer, the sun <u>did</u> come out! Hooray! However, I had neglected to say anything about the <u>rain</u>, so rain kept falling and falling while the sun was out. God was having fun with me. It was if he were saying, "El, you're supposed to be the lawyer, but you forgot to command the rain to stop. Hahaha." The joke was definitely on me.

Another one: We were getting ready to sell our house on Angelo Drive and move to Huntingdon. After heavy rains some people on our street were having drainage problems. Lines of pipe were showing up on their lawns, pumping water into the street. I was getting worried about the appearance of the street while we were trying to sell our house. The weather eventually cleared, and the pipes went away.

A while after that, more torrential rains came. I asserted authority over the situation in the name of Jesus and commanded everything to work right so that people didn't have to pump out their basements and have those pipes all over their lawns. It worked. There were no pipes or drains in view on Angelo Drive again while we lived there.

Later on, in Huntingdon I took authority for a small, really petty, reason. I had to go a few houses down the street to help a neighbor at 1:30 PM, and I simply didn't want to walk in the rain. At noon it was raining cats and dogs. I was just too lazy to carry an umbrella. I prayed and it continued to pour, even increasing. I stood firm. At 1:29 the rain completely ceased. No lie. Power of God.

The most humorous of all these weather-related stories I save for last. I have witnesses for this one. All or most of us Elders at Living Waters were gathered at the Hampton townhouse of Elder Keith Keoppel one day. It may have been after church; I can't remember. The deck had a beautiful display of flowers and potted plants, and we were eating outside. The weather grew threatening. A big, dark storm cloud was coming our way. We were Elders of a Charismatic church, and believed in the power of God over just about anything. We went after that storm cloud and in agreement commanded that cloud to GO AWAY IN JESUS'S NAME! Guess what happened. It did go away, and we were not soaked with rain.

God got the last laugh on that one, however, just like the other one I mentioned about the sun coming out. In our enthusiasm, we hadn't thought to specify where we wanted that cloud to go. When Pastor Tom got home to his townhouse in Hamburg, he found his place soaked! I can't prove it, but it sounds as if that nasty rain cloud had found its way to <u>his</u> house!

If you want more.

You can check out my articles for Cross Rhythms.

At one time I had a folder called "Everyday Miracles," trying to record events like these. I felt the Lord saying, however (as an impression), "Don't worry about it, El; you won't be able to keep up with me." That having been said, my personal view is that such acts of God don't happen all the time in big, dramatic ways except in certain seasons. At least that's my experience. Nevertheless, if we try to stay close to the Lord throughout the day, every day, talking to Him and listening for Him, we can feel the Holy Spirit guiding us. I'm not tuned in to this as much as some other Christians, but I'm getting better. You'll see an example in the next Chapter, when we leave Sparta for Huntingdon, PA.

On a farm outside of Huntingdon, PA.

47

Sparta, NJ to Huntingdon, PA?

As I start this Chapter something hit me. I've been recounting the miraculous in a book that itself might be characterized as miraculous, thanks to the power of God. I'm this far into my memoirs, and started writing it only 20 days ago. That time period includes a few days when, after a burst of initial energy, I gave up on the idea.

The period also includes the inordinate amount of time I spent on formatting, and playing with font types and sizes. (Most of the time was wasted, since the Publisher and I went another route later.) As I make that confession to you, I am reminded of a wonderful song by singer-songwriter John Gorka, called "Land of the Bottom Line," on his 1990 album of the same name. It contains the great line "All I ever wanted was to be a kid and play." He could have added "with fonts on MS Word each day."

Back to business; serious business. After ten years in a big house in Sparta, Sheila and I thought of downsizing. The failure of my old law firm accelerated that thought process. I was thinking about the possibility of moving to the next town over, Byram, when Sheila said, "What about Huntingdon?"

To be honest, it wasn't on my radar screen at the time. I had left Huntingdon in 1963 to attend Mt. Hermon. My mother had been such a big part of the town that when we would visit, it always felt as if we were visiting <u>her</u> town. Sheila and I were married there and had a lot of affection for the town, so we decided to "seek confirmation" that God wanted us to relocate to Huntingdon.

Let me share with you my testimony (in substantial part), written in 2012, about the move:

El Testimony: 2012 Return to Huntingdon, PA

I believe that Sheila and I were called to Huntingdon, and this is my testimony:

In May 2012, by reason of a number of circumstances, Sheila and I concluded that we wanted to downsize. We had a large house that accommodated our four children and us, but the former had flown the coop. We used barely a third of the house on a regular basis.

I started searching for property in a nearby town, where the taxes were lower. One Sunday, upon my return from church (which was Living Waters Fellowship, a church of which I was one of nine co-founders), I spoke with Sheila on this subject. She then uttered the now-famous words, "What about Huntingdon?" We had looked into relocating to Huntingdon in 2002, but it did not seem to be the right move back then. In 2012, I hadn't even thought about Huntingdon as a possibility, and was intrigued that the idea came from Sheila.

I had a historical connection with Huntingdon, since my mother, sister and I moved here from Lewistown in 1960; I had friends and relatives here and nearby; and Sheila and I had been married in St. James Lutheran Church in 1971.

Yet, it was a town in which the strongest family presence here had been my mother, and I had, in essence, been a visitor since the mid-1960's, when I went away to secondary school, college and law school.

So, what to do? Sheila and I decided to seek "confirmation" of the "rightness" of the move. We were both heavily involved in church matters at two separate churches, and I had been leading for over five years a weekly Christian fellowship group at a housing facility in Newton, NJ, the county seat. Moreover, two of our children were in NJ. A move to Huntingdon would be a major change.

In May 2012 we came to Huntingdon for a visit, and received what I consider to be confirmation from the Holy Spirit for our move. As we came into town, the first person I saw on the street was none other than Christine Reed, who was my mother's primary caretaker for many years, and was with my mother when she died.

After speaking with Chris, we went to visit another beloved Chris -- Chris Dunbar at First National Bank. The latter Chris had managed my mother's checkbook and financial affairs with great dedication and loyalty in mother's declining years. When Chris Dunbar found out that we were staying at the Fairfield Inn, she mentioned an employee there who previously had worked at our newspaper, The Daily News.

The next morning Sheila and I sought out that lady (whose name, sadly, escapes me), and had a very enjoyable conversation with her. We then went back to our breakfast. A little while later the lady returned, and shared this with us. She told us that her husband's parents had worked for my grandparents, the Joseph Biddles (my mother's parents), on 5th Street during the Depression, and but for the kindness of the Biddles, they might not have had enough to eat. That testimony moved and blessed Sheila and me.

The final piece of confirmation was this: we drove out Fairgrounds Road to look at the Victoria Manor and Cree developments. At Victoria, there was a young man on the street, so I rolled down the window and asked him whether he lived there and whether he liked it. As I was about to leave, I had an impulse (still, small voice?) to ask him his name. He looked at me and said "El Biddle." That young man was the son of my first-cousin Andy Biddle! The only person on the street in that development at that time was my cousin!

We <u>were</u> called to Huntingdon, and it has been a joy walking out this call, with tremendous fruit already.

48

Indeed, Sparta to Huntingdon!

After we moved to Sparta in 2002, I would make dramatic statements like "I won't be leaving Angelo Drive except on a gurney." Sheila said she'd never move again. Ever. The Lord can certainly make categorical statements look foolish in retrospect.

Ten years later, in October 2012, the moving trucks came, the men loaded our stuff, and off they went to Huntingdon, PA. We, on the other hand, had to wait for the Vet. She seemed to be the only person on earth capable of getting our cat Fritz into the cat carrier. (The other cat Scotty was more manageable.) It took her thirty seconds and we paid her $100. That dwarfed even my lofty billing rate at LeBoeuf, Lamb, but it was worth it. We were off on our adventure back to "God's country, central PA region."

As I sit here now and reflect on the five years we spent in my old stomping grounds, the period seems somewhat like a hiatus or interregnum, or something less grandiose, like recess at school. That was not our intent at all in moving. As discussed above, I felt called to Huntingdon. Moreover, it was such an ingenious call, coming through Sheila. As I reasoned later, if God did indeed call us to Huntingdon, doing it through Sheila was brilliant. The reason was that if it had been my idea, and later on became a disaster, I might well have beaten myself up. I would say that, rather than God's idea, the whole thing had been some nostalgic and misguided idea of mine. Since the idea came from Sheila, that couldn't happen.

My return to Huntingdon put to the test the aphorism associated with Thomas Wolfe that you "can't go home again." At first, I rejected it. I reveled in driving around all my old haunts, the high school, and Lewistown, McConnellstown, and Williamsburg (the real one, not that fancy place in Virginia). I even got ambitious and drove down to Calvin and Cassville. They may not be household names, but they appear on any "good" map of PA. I looked up old high-school friends and even attended the 50th reunion of my class at the high school from which I didn't graduate.

Sheila and I visited extensively with my Biddle relatives, and saw my cousins Harry, Elliot, and Molly Biddle perform in high school activities and grow up before our eyes, eventually graduating high school as High-Honors recipients, with Molly as class Valedictorian.

We also enjoyed getting reconnected with the Ron and Barb Detwilers, family friends who had the distinction of liking my music even more than I did, and purchasing more of it than anybody else, with the possible exception of a fellow in Japan one time.

What did become clear to me after a while was that maybe you could go "home" again, but you couldn't go home to your youth again. That realization was a bit of a downer, bringing again to mind John Gorka's line "all I ever wanted was to be a kid and play." All the people I wanted to play with were old, when I wasn't (or so I claimed).

The "fruit" of the Huntingdon experience was sometimes not of the local variety. I did the book with Steve Baughman in 2013, and then a joke book in 2014, to which Steve contributed a quirky Foreword that was as good as the book. In 2015 I wrote a book for Mel Bay Publications called "The Art of Gospel Guitar."

Sheila and I did have some local success with our entries in the illustrious (really!) Huntingdon County Fair. Sheila scored more blue ribbons than I did, but I got some for my shellcraft. The best thing I ever did, however, received only a Third, and I'm still grumpy about that.

I took a shot at establishing some local ministries, but came up short. I invented something called the "Huntingdon Hat Ministry." I was concerned that people around town didn't seem to dress that warm in the winter. I purchased and distributed a bunch of hats, and people were blessed. After a while, however, everybody seemed to <u>have</u> a hat, or they did things incomprehensible to me, like wearing shorts in February. I retired the "Huntingdon Hat Ministry," concluding that people in Huntingdon were just a hardier sort than my wimpy friends in New Jersey.

I thought about another ministry at an apartment building in Mt. Union run by a Godly fellow. That went awry almost immediately when a resident there categorically announced that getting "slain in the Spirit" wasn't biblical. (Hel-lo. If that were true, why did everyone think the boys and girls in the upper room at Pentecost in Acts 2 had been hitting the wine-skins?)

Sheila and I attended Stone Church of the Brethren, associated with Juniata College and with which I had a fond connection. My Huntingdon friend, the late Bruce Kauffman, was the son of Stewart Kauffman, who had been the pastor there in the 1960's. Bruce's house had been right across from the church, and we had lots of good times there.

Stone, however, was unabashedly a "seeker-sensitive" church, and I was a "full-gospel" kind of guy. I came to attend Word of Life Fellowship on the outskirts of town. Despite its acronym of "WOLF," which bothered me a little but nobody else, it was a great church. It had all the attributes mentioned at the end of Chapter 45, not that I had any list then or was checking it twice.

The pastor there Steve Watkins was a humble and prayerful Spirit-filled guy, with the highest view of Scripture. He preached well, rode a motorcycle, piloted a plane, and actually knew how to fix cars. He also had a prayer warrior of a wife, beautiful on the inside and outside, as well as Godly Elders and Deacons, and a bunch of other devil-kickers of whom I remain very fond.

I seemed to be the only lawyer at the church. It was OK. I didn't get the impression they had run others out of town.

At the church I found myself doing theretofore unheard of (for me) things like attending a men's Sunday School class. That class was led by Jim Kyper, who has one heck of an exhortation anointing on him. I even went to Wednesday night prayer meetings and the monthly men's prayer meetings on Thursdays. I hadn't done things like that even at the church of which I was one of the founders!

I got myself baptized by immersion by Pastor Steve. I created some amusement in the crowd by whining a bit about the water being cold in the swimming pool that was serving as our version of the Jordan River.

I had some talented guitar students in Huntingdon, including Jared Pilch, Robbie Goss, Andrew Garman, and Joan Coppes. Jared made great progress in the CGDGAD tuning, bringing to it a groove and flow that were uniquely his own.

Sheila was having a good time in Huntingdon, absorbed in her usual activities of reading, knitting, crocheting, solving impossible (for me) cryptic puzzles, and contributing to the life of Stone Church. On the culinary front, we went early and often for dinner at the best restaurant in three or four counties, Mimi's in Huntingdon. We became mainstays at a favorite table in the corner of the "Fine Dining" area. There we could spy on the bar area, while eavesdropping on people in our room. Mimi's was established and run by Rhonda ("Mimi") Muir and her husband, my classmate Jamie Muir.

I became very friendly with Jamie's older brother Jay Muir, each of us claiming to keep the other out of trouble.

In the fifth year of our somewhat idyllic existence in Huntingdon, two things happened. First, as I said to Sheila one time, "There are only so many times I can drive to Cassville." More importantly, it hit us that we simply wanted to be closer to our children and grandchildren. I can testify when and where that hit me: I was driving up the hill into Taylor Highlands toward our home in August of 2017. A couple of weeks later, on a Sunday, I was returning from "WOLF" and got a more refined word. This time I believe it was from the Lord. It wasn't an audible voice of

God, but I remember the words: "Your children need you." That was pretty heavy.

I had to water-drop on Sheila about this. She was settled in Huntingdon. She liked Huntingdon and had friends there, as did I. She also understood, however, that we were isolated from the children. She was keenly aware of the seven-hours-one-way hike to see daughter Mary, husband Josh Kohan, and granddaughter Evelyn in Albany, New York. All the McMeens were within striking distance from Sparta, NJ, but not Huntingdon: Jon and Erin McMeen, in Sparta; Dan and Lyndsay McMeen, in Red Bank, NJ; the aforesaid Kohans in Albany; and Jim and Marissa McMeen, and son Conner (and now daughter Kelsey), in Yardley, PA.

Our experience proves the adage that if you dwell on the impossible, it becomes inevitable. We were going back to Sparta. For the third time in the 21st Century Sheila and I packed up a house.

Before leaving town, however, I had to address some questions. Why had we been "called" back to Huntingdon in the first place? Was it "right" for us to leave? In the words of Humphrey Bogart in the movie "Casablanca," we were just "two little people" in a world full of problems. Still, these matters were important to me.

I believe that Sheila and I blessed folks in Huntingdon in a lot of ways, in a lot of quarters. I've already mentioned in Chapter 40 my association with Pastor Denny Hunsinger. I also name my high school classmate Pastor Tim Shafer here. As to others, I won't name names, but some people reading this far in the book will know who they are. The Lord put us in your path for reasons that we may not fully know until Glory. Sheila blessed Stone Church and I WOLF. As to the latter, I have shared with Pastor Steve and Michelle Watkins my thinking on that subject, fragmentary as it must be until I meet Jesus face-to-face.

The blessings went both ways. Sheila and I were blessed by many people in Huntingdon. They included my relatives, of course, and the Ron Detwilers, Amy Dell Hess, Christine Reed, the WOLF pack (including, notably, Elder Les Cregger), the people at Stone Church, Jay Muir, Marcie Muir, Scott Burnett of Car Care in Huntingdon – too many to name.

In my case, I may simply have needed rest after the ministry in Newton, NJ. The thought has crossed my mind that the Lord plucked me out of Brookside Terrace and Living Waters at just the right time for me. The Lord, in addition, put people in front of me in Huntingdon who encouraged me, including the people at WOLF and my guitar students.

There is one more thing. Early on in our Huntingdon period I was listening to a sermon on the "Jubilee," from the Old Testament. In the 49th year, each person was called to return to his clan, and thereafter proclaim liberty to all the inhabitants. If I essentially left Huntingdon in 1963, the 49th year put me smack into 2012, the precise year we moved from Sparta to Huntingdon! I'd like to think that I did proclaim the gospel of Jesus Christ to my beloved clan in Huntingdon, and to many other people, too.

Says it all.

49

Back to Sparta

I've written too much of this book at night. I'm tired. Plus, I have this image burned into my brain of me typing away in the wee hours while our cat Millie sleeps peacefully on the bed behind my desk. That's OK; she's the best, most affectionate and playful little cat we've ever had (or, since she's a cat, I should say ever "served"). See below.

As I conclude this book, I realize that it's not really a "memoir." It's more like a guided tour of my life, led by me, with running commentary about the tour itself. I hope it worked for you.

We have moved into a house in Sparta that served for a season as a "Chabad." That means the glory of God. What an encouraging start to our new Chapter, and this concluding one!

I shall let you go, spare you more text, and conclude simply with a recent picture of Sheila and me, taken at a favorite restaurant of ours, Casa Bellisima in Andover, NJ.

Thanks for joining us on the tour!

CPSIA information can be obtained
at www.ICGtesting.com
Printed in the USA
BVHW07s1035081018
529574BV00003B/311/P